JOHN WHITING

Saint's Day

WITH AN INTRODUCTION BY
E. R. WOOD

HEINEMANN EDUCATIONAL
BOOKS LTD · LONDON

Heinemann Educational Books Ltd
LONDON EDINBURGH MELBOURNE TORONTO
SINGAPORE JOHANNESBURG AUCKLAND
IBADAN HONG KONG NAIROBI
NEW DELHI

ISBN 0 435 22942 7

Saint's Day first published
in *Plays of the Year* (Paul Elek) 1953
and then in *The Plays of John Whiting* (Heinemann) 1957
First published in *The Hereford Plays* 1963
Reprinted 1965, 1971

Published by
Heinemann Educational Books Ltd
48 Charles Street, London W1X 8AH
Printed Offset Litho in Great Britain by
Cox & Wyman Ltd,
London, Fakenham and Reading

INTRODUCTION

JOHN WHITING was born at Salisbury in 1917, educated at Taunton School, and trained as an actor at the Royal Academy of Dramatic Art. He served in the army throughout the last war, after which he worked in the theatre, acting mainly in repertory at Harrogate and York. He wrote most of *Saint's Day* in 1948, but it was not performed until 1951. In that year the Arts Theatre Club organized a play competition to celebrate the Festival of Britain and offered a prize of £700 for the best new play. There were nearly a thousand entries, from which the judges—Alec Clunes, Christopher Fry and Peter Ustinov—chose three to be tried out in performance. The last to be performed was *Saint's Day*, and the judges chose this as the winner in spite of the bewildered reception that it suffered on the first night. John Whiting was not unknown, for earlier in 1951 *A Penny for a Song* had been presented at the Haymarket Theatre, where in spite of excellent production (by Peter Brook) and acting, it had had only a short run. After *Saint's Day* came *Marching Song* (1954). None of these plays was a commercial success in the theatre, but they established a reputation for their author as a disturbing playwright of original talent. When in 1961 *The Devils* was presented by the Royal Shakespeare Company at the Aldwych Theatre, it was received with general enthusiasm.

John Whiting's plays are concerned with human problems such as war, violence and intolerance, but he raised questions without offering solutions. Neither as a writer nor as a citizen did he reveal any commitment to political parties or causes. He found 'movements' too constricting; he wanted to treat problems from a personal point of view; he said that he was 'one of that disappearing species, a private individual'.

When he died in June 1963, *The Times* said: 'The British Theatre, even in its present flowering, can ill afford to lose the plays he might have written had he lived long enough to achieve his full potential stature'.

John Whiting and the Contemporary Theatre

In 1951 *Saint's Day* ran for only three weeks. It was harshly attacked by leading critics,[1] though such distinguished men of the theatre as Sir Tyrone Guthrie and Sir John Gielgud wrote to *The Times* in its defence. Yet when the play was revived ten years later at the Birmingham Repertory Theatre the audience appeared to follow it with appreciation and without bewilderment. Evidently a change had taken place in public taste and awareness, so that playgoers were in tune by 1961 with something that was too original in 1951.

The English theatre has often been slow to reflect the spirit of the age, and in 1951 audiences were accustomed to plays which took little account of the immense changes in values and beliefs that the war years had brought. In France the writings of Sartre and Camus had already begun to express the collapse of faith in religious and humanist ideals that has since become familiar throughout Europe, but in England theatregoers were still enjoying plays that could have been written thirty years before. No wonder they were not ready for *Saint's Day*.

John Whiting upset the composure of audiences not merely because some of his characters voiced unfamiliar patterns of thought, but because the message of the play as a whole seemed obscure or ambivalent. The playgoer expected to be able to say to himself by the end of the first act: 'I know roughly what kind of play this is. I can see the author's intentions shaping; I recognize the problems put before us, and I can see which characters are on our side.' He was accustomed to a type of play that was a survival from the age of Shaw and Galsworthy. Even an iconoclastic writer like Shaw, who had once shocked and annoyed audiences by his paradoxical and sometimes heretical ideas, had left them in no doubt about which character was the author's spokesman or about what conclusions he was putting before them at the end. Moreover, he was able to put forward

[1] The kindest critic was J. C. Trewin, who wrote: 'I came into the clanging street, angry and baffled, unable to shed the weight of that dark house, that world of query and symbol. I wondered whether it could be right to dismiss as turgid nonsense a play that had so powerful an effect on the mind, one that would not release its hold.'

his conclusions with great confidence. It seemed then that convincing answers existed to the questions raised. John Whiting belongs to a different age, when the very solutions of the old problems seem to have produced new and more difficult ones; when the playwright does not claim to 'know the answers'. We may nowadays look back with envy on a time when a bright future for mankind seemed to depend on good sense and goodwill.

Since John Whiting wrote his first three plays, a revolution in ideas and methods has transformed the English theatre, or at least that small but influential part of it that is more than entertainment industry. In some ways he was a forerunner of the change; and to some extent he has benefited from the new climate that others have created. Some people would say that the new era began with the production in 1955 of Samuel Beckett's *Waiting for Godot*: others date it from John Osborne's *Look Back in Anger*, produced at the Royal Court Theatre in 1956; other important events in 1956 were the visit of the Berliner Ensemble to perform plays by Bertolt Brecht, and the emergence of Joan Littlewood as director of Theatre Workshop. The next few years saw the production of many new plays by new playwrights, not all commercial successes, not all masterpieces, but all contributing to an impression of exciting creative energy. Amidst the new ferment of contemporary drama, critics have tried to distinguish three trends associated with the influences mentioned above. The first may be indicated by the title of an essay by Martin Esslin, *Godot and His Children*; the second in the book *Anger and After*, by J. R. Taylor. The third trend is the Brechtian influence. If such trends really exist as important features of the theatre of today, it must be said that John Whiting belongs to none of them, either as a forerunner or as a follower. He has least in common with the so-called Social Realism initiated by *Look Back in Anger*; rather more with writers like Beckett and Pinter. It would be an exaggeration to suggest that *Saint's Day* was a forerunner of *Waiting for Godot*; but there is some resemblance in the psychological landscape and the atmosphere. Playgoers who have travelled since through the Beckett and Pinter country would hardly complain of obscurity in *Saint's Day*. *Godot* and its successors have helped audiences to catch up with John Whiting.

When *The Devils* was performed in 1961 by the Royal Shakespeare Company, a critic wrote in the *New Statesman*: 'In any view it is, with all its faults, easily the nearest English drama has got to a great tragedy for 300 years or more' and he went on to praise 'the sustained imagination of its highly personal style, the fluidity of its kaleidoscopic action, and the irony and audacity of its conception'. The reader who recalls what the critics originally said of *Saint's Day* may see here some measure of the degree to which John Whiting has come into his own.

Themes of Saint's Day

The main theme of *Saint's Day* is responsibility for violence and suffering. The play was written only a few years after the dropping of the first atom bomb on Hiroshima (August 6, 1945). By then the full horror of this attack, in which 78,000 people were killed, had come to be realized; the relief at the end of the war had faded; and the question was troubling men's consciences: who was responsible? Could we place responsibility on the men who flew the plane, the senior officers who gave the orders, the President of the United States as Commander-in-Chief, the peoples of the Atlantic Alliance to whom it brought quick victory, the Japanese war-lords who had brought their country into the war with the treacherous attack on Pearl Harbour, the Japanese officers in charge of camps in which Allied prisoners of war had received inhuman treatment, the people of Hiroshima itself, in whose name these atrocities had been committed, or on an unconscious impulse to violence in all men? Similar questions had been provoked by the trials of Nazi leaders accused of crimes on a scale previously unheard-of in history. Such problems of responsibility must continue to disturb anyone who is awake to events in the world today. In *Saint's Day* the appalling events concern a small group of people, but throughout the play we are aware of the wider significance.

The incidents are of three kinds: there is the type that begins in comparatively harmless foolery and ends in disaster, not consciously intended or foreseen, like the shooting of Stella; there is the kind of action which is intentionally vindictive, though having consequences extending beyond what was willed by the initiators, like the breaking of Aldus; and there is the atrocity which soldiers like Melrose will carry out if somebody gives the orders and takes the responsibility. The question of responsibility repeatedly arises. National and international affairs provide numerous parallels. Throughout the play one has a sense of two levels, the individual and realistic on the one hand, and the general and apocalyptic on the other. We see disaster come to a group of individuals, and this may be an image of what is in store for the world.

Linked with this theme of responsibility is an exploration of the springs of the will to destruction. Paul and Charles have withdrawn from the world from different motives, but they are at one in their contempt for mankind and their obsession with hostility. Their quarrel with the village begins as a melodramatic and even hilarious game, but it ends in catastrophe. Stella warns them of this. When Paul hears that three soldiers have escaped from prison and attacked the village, he proposes to form an alliance with them. Stella's 'sudden storm of foreknowledge' in which she speaks of the approaching 'point of deviation' and the 'call from another room' is a premonition that they will bring disaster on themselves. In a wider sense it is a warning to humanity; the human race is all one; those who play at hostilities bring destruction on themselves; they cannot ultimately escape what goes on in 'another room'. Paul is so blinded by the old antagonism that he is not diverted from his course of self-destruction. In the crucial scene with Aldus he reaffirms his plan. However contemptible Aldus may seem to Paul and Charles, he is a man in distress appealing on behalf of others for help against the forces of lawlessness represented by the soldiers. There is simple dignity in his words: 'I know the history of hatred, sir, and yet I appeal to you in my weakness for help against these men.' Paul will not see that the soldiers are a threat to everybody; he is so ready to relish his old game of war with the village that he replies: 'I shall form an alliance, but it will be with the soldiers, and with them I shall revenge myself upon you and your impudent mob.' Nobody will help Aldus against the dark forces that are to overwhelm them all. Stella does make a feeble gesture of sympathy; Procathren is out of his depth; Charles laughs; Paul makes Aldus repeat his appeal so that he may reject it the more brutally. Only later, when he is confronted with the realities of violence, does Paul Southman learn wisdom, and then it is too late.

The change in Procathren is more extraordinary. At the outset he is timid and conventional, accustomed to 'run from the event'; but after the shock of the accidental shooting of Stella he becomes ruthlessly and aggressively destructive. This kind of reaction, puzzling in an individual, may be more familiar in terms of national attitudes and group ideologies. The modern world has seen the collapse of faith, first in religion and then in humanism, as a result of the massive shocks inflicted by man's appalling inhumanity to man in the last quarter century. The ensuing nihilism offers prospects of infinitely greater destruction. It resembles in a wider sphere the personal crisis of Procathren. He had lost his faith in God years ago, but still thought we were here on earth 'to do well by each other' (a humanist view). When Paul and Charles take from him his faith in man, he can see nothing but darkness and beyond it darkness. Life has ceased to have meaning. What mankind needs is tenderness, love, but Procathren now says that 'the thing's played out'. He regards death as a release, and arranges the killing of Paul and Charles as if it were an offer of freedom. Beyond his own troubles he recognizes 'the clamour of voices crying out against the end'. If this vision of Procathren's is a dark glimpse of a coming world without faith, a world that has lost its innocence, then it is a chilling thought that the man who is most at home in it is Melrose, who cares for nothing, who says, 'Nobody's anything to me', who will kill without a qualm. He resembles Bruno Hurst in *Marching Song*. Such men are thrown up by war and violence; they may be destined to inherit the future.

But the outlook of the play is not entirely dark. Paul Southman learns (though, like King Lear, too late) the importance of compassion. At the end he tries to offer to the refugee child the tenderness that was lacking in his relations with his grand-daughter; and he welcomes the villagers with good-neighbourly sympathy in place of his old antagonism. The conversion does not save him, but it is surely an essential strand in the meaning of the play. The response of the villagers is mainly unspoken; but as far as they are concerned, the ancient feud is clearly forgotten, if, indeed, it ever existed for ordinary people. They are no adherents of warring factions, but a group of human beings drawn together by misfortune. The response of the child is unconscious, but significant. She acknowledges Paul's overtures of kindliness with faltering signals of contact, such as taking up his copy of *Alice in Wonderland* and picking up the scarf that he dropped. She is unaware enough to perform a grave dance while the ominous trumpet sounds, but at the end she senses the atmosphere and hides her face in her mother's lap. The author has been at pains to avoid anything sentimental in the figure of the child, but he uses her to bring the play to an end on an inarticulate note of compassion.

There are a number of other recurring themes in the play. Fear and cruelty are as common in the Southman household as in international relations. Much of Paul's fear is plainly irrational. It is difficult to believe that the villagers have ever intended to attack the house, molest John Winter on his shopping outings, or poison the dog. Stella is infected with this fear, which has shadowed her life. Cruelty is strangely mingled with love: Paul, Stella and Charles are frequently cruel to those they care for.

The play contains much speculation on death and the purpose of life. Different characters at different times think of life as an adventure and death as an enemy to be fought; of death as something to be feared because of what may be revealed by the light; of death as darkness with nothing but darkness beyond; of life as a preparation for the nothingness of death; and of life as an opportunity to accumulate memories to provide the material of existence in death. Nobody suggests here (as the Victorian optimists did) that life is a splendid boon or death a great adventure.

A minor theme of the play is the standing of the artist in the community. There is a corrective here to the comfortable assumption that writers and painters are of their nature wise prophets, unacknowledged legislators, inspirers of the noblest in man. Southman and Heberden are bitter castigators of society; their scorn may be stimulating and astringent, but it is destructive. A community might well have misgivings about the influence of artists who do not believe in humanity or in life. Art as a fashionable accomplishment may be even less healthy: culture-worshippers such as Procathren help the shams to flourish in society. Aldus is another of them. When these artists see through themselves they cannot stand the revelation.

The title, *Saint's Day*, is a pointer to the meaning of the play. January 25, Paul Southman's birthday and also the day of his death, is the date celebrated as that of St Paul's conversion. St Paul, a noted persecutor of Christians, literally saw the light on that day, and was converted to the very faith he had been attacking. When Stella speaks of Paul Southman's 'saintliness', the link with St Paul appears to be ironic; but later Paul says, 'It's a very great day for me, this birthday of mine;' it is the day of his conversion to a new attitude to his fellow-men. The force of what happens is blunted by Paul's apparent mental breakdown; but in his 'tower of senility and lunacy', which so angers Charles, he is certainly groping towards the faith he had once denied.

When the themes of the play are considered and analysed, as in the foregoing pages, it is not suggested that the author said to himself, 'I am going to write a play about responsibility' or any of the other themes mentioned above, any more than Shakespeare, before writing the Histories, can be supposed to have first crystallized his theories of kingship. As it happens, John Whiting revealed, in an interview with the magazine *Encore*, the starting point of the play:

It was a place, actually, and a mural in a house. A place where I was in the army—which is probably the reason for the soldiers in the play. It was in the early part of the war, in the Midlands somewhere. It was winter and it was miserable. We had nothing to burn, so we went out to see if we could find a house we could tear down. In quite large grounds we came across this obviously derelict house. We went in; there were no lights and we had to use torches. And *there* was this most extraordinary painting on the wall. . . . Standing there in that house, I suddenly had the most extraordinary feeling, which stayed with me for six years.

The strangeness of this experience probably accounts for the special atmosphere of the play, a quality which stirs the imagination with mysterious reverberations.

But the author was, always much concerned with questions of responsibility—*Marching Song* deals with aspects of it—and when he began to people his strange house with characters in a situation, the theme developed from them. A play is not a manifesto; its purpose is not to teach truths but to communicate an experience in terms of theatre. But worthwhile plays are usually *about something*; important plays are about something important.

The Characters

Though *Saint's Day* is important as a play of ideas, in that it raises disturbing questions of prophetic significance for the world, all the ideas spring from consideration of the people in it. These characters are not the stock figures of the conventional theatre, in which, at its crudest, there is no difficulty in recognizing at sight the 'hero' and the 'villain'. Such characterization depends on a simplified view of human beings, which can be convenient in the theatre, both for the actors to present and for the audience to react to. But one of the developments of recent years has been towards a less predictable presentation of character, and of this *Saint's Day* was a forerunner. We fluctuate in our response to the people in this play as different aspects of their natures claim our understanding; at one time we are on Southman's side; at another Stella most stirs our sympathy; our contempt for Procathren changes to mingled revulsion and compassion. They are all both right and wrong.

Just as the characters themselves evoke from us varying responses at different times, so in their relations with each other there is a changing and paradoxical compound of love-hate, cruelty-tenderness, fear-arrogance. In the Southman household the business of living together and loving each other is very difficult.

Paul Southman is the most dominating person in the play and theatrically the most powerful creation. One might have expected this to become one of the famous roles for great actors to aspire to. He has once been 'a real turtle', a famous man and a force to be feared in the great world. He may remind the reader of Jonathan Swift (1667–1745), who similarly exiled himself from the society in which he had been so eminent, and spent his life in lashing mankind with bitter satire until his towering intellect crumbled into the misery of madness. It is perhaps not a coincidence that Southman's grand-daughter is called Stella; for Swift is known to have cared in his stormy life for two women; and one of them, to whom he wrote a celebrated series of letters and whom he may have secretly married, was known to him as Stella. The character of Southman bears some resemblance also to Ezra Pound, the distinguished American poet. Pound too was an angry pamphleteer; his disgust with the economic injustices and follies of the democracies in the 'thirties led him to alliance with its enemies. He worked for Fascist Italy in the war of 1939–45 against his own country, and when he was eventually taken prisoner he was spared the usual fate of traitors only by being judged to be insane and imprisoned in a mental hospital. Madness is a point of resemblance in all three; Paul Southman takes refuge in madness at the end, like many tragic heroes from Shakespeare to Pirandello, when he cannot face himself and the consequences of his acts.

This ageing misanthrope has been accustomed to wielding power, though now he can flaunt his authority only over John Winter. 'John Winter is my servant,' he says, 'and he shall obey my orders.' His fantasy of waging war on the village offers opportunities to indulge his illusions of command: he generously dismisses doubts of Winter's loyalty and congratulates him on 'an excellent and lucid report'. Stella tells the pair of them to stop playing at being soldiers: 'This is no time', she exclaims, 'to indulge in your fancy for campaigning.' But although his military talk is ridiculous, it has an exciting quality of turbulence and dramatic power on the stage. So also he is impressive in his magnificent scorn of his inferiors, even when he lashes such feeble victims as Aldus and Procathren appear to be. In this he has some of Swift's stature, and the same saving quality of including himself in his ironical mockery.

Only occasionally in the early part of the play do we see glimpses of threatening senility. Stella needs to tell him to wipe his nose on one occasion, and his tears on another; he has moments when he is frightened of meeting Procathren or of attending the dinner where he may disgrace himself; and he wishes he had some better clothes. At such times we are touched by the spectacle of greatness dwindling into the helplessness of old age.

Up to the crisis this turbulent old fighter shows little to justify Stella's attribution to him of 'saintliness'. ('You have proved your integrity and saintliness, and tonight it is that they will honour.') Even within the family he is deficient in sympathy; he is mainly interested in himself and his past quarrels; he appears to be unaware of Stella's profound unhappiness. His deepest care is not for his grand-daughter but his dog. Outside the family he enjoys conflict. Attention has already been drawn to crucial occasions when his decisions or actions turn the course of events in a fatal direction. There is irony in his confidence that he is in the right each time that he wilfully takes the wrong course. When Stella warns him of the 'point of deviation', he replies, 'We are very much aware of the menace of the point of deviation. We are eagerly awaiting the shout from another room, for we know from whom it will come and to whom it will be directed.' When later he rejects Aldus's appeal for help he describes it as 'an awful display of fear, non-comprehension and self-conscious pathos'—words that could appropriately be applied to his own attitude. When he and Charles laughingly describe to Procathren the stages of firing the pistol he little knows how prophetically true are his words 'and down comes the house that Paul built'. When the train of events that he has set in motion leads to the burning of the village he asks, 'Who is responsible?' and when Charles says it was an accident he voices the main theme of the play with his words: 'There is always the responsibility—it must rest with someone.' A large part of it rests, of course, with Paul himself.

At the crisis there is a profound change, more like the transformation of King Lear than the conversion of St Paul. At first he cannot believe that Stella is dead; then, having placed the responsibility on Procathren, he forgives him; but the 'terrible spasm of grief and fear' changes him into a different man. All his old fire leaves him. He is anxious to forgive. He would like to have children around him. He is groping for tenderness. When Procathren expresses the agony of his loss of faith in life, Paul silently takes his hand, as if to show his understanding and sympathy. How much of his madness is a refuge and how much an affliction is not precisely determined; but he appears to be wiser in his madness than when he was considered sane. If he had realized earlier the importance of human relations, he might have seen more meaning in life, and not laid himself open to Procathren's accusation of 'knowing that it is not a question of finding but of losing the pieties, the allegiances, the loves'. At the end he is trying to find them again.

The author of *Saint's Day* has said that it is about self-destruction. (So are *Marching Song* and *The Devils*; so, for that matter, are most tragedies.) Certainly Paul Southman brings destruction on himself. His withdrawal from the world is the first stage of decline; it is followed by his long feud with the villagers; his rejection of Aldus's appeal for help is the culmination. When Charles and Paul set out to break the personality of Procathren, the envoy of the world they have turned from, they provoke a crisis in him which ultimately brings on them brutal retribution. Charles curses Paul when he abdicates responsibility: 'God damn you for the beastliness—the selfishness of shutting yourself up in your tower of senility and lunacy at this moment!' But it is the earlier shutting himself up in his tower of misanthropy that began it all, and at the end of the play Paul seems to have realized this.

The crisis that stills the storm in Paul Southman has a different effect on Robert Procathren, (whose name includes a Greek element that refers to purgation through suffering). Up to the killing of Stella he has been an ingratiating hanger-on to artists of greater talent than his own, so lacking in discrimination that he is impressed by Aldus because he has a lot of books. We share the contempt of Charles and Paul, though we must feel some sympathy for him in his well-meant efforts to honour the great man in eclipse, when he meets with such embarrassing rebuffs. His slightly patronizing efforts to take an interest in Charles Heberden are coldly received; Charles is a genuine artist who is contemptuously indifferent to public recognition: in contrast, Robert Procathren is a minor critic and poet whose photograph is found in magazines, and who mixes with fashionable people. We soon find that he prefers his personal relations to be fairly shallow: he is horrified at the prospect of becoming involved in other people's troubles. He has never handled a weapon and has never 'run towards the event'.

The striking scene in which Charles and Paul, half-laughing, half-malicious, ridicule and humiliate Procathren as they did Aldus, is built up to the random and accidental (but strangely foredoomed) shot that kills Stella. After the first numb horror he accepts responsibility, assumes a ruthless authority, and 'runs toward the event'. He incites Aldus to burn his books (a symbolic denial of religion), he goes through the burning village with the lawless soldiers, talking volubly to people who cannot understand him, and finally comes back to order the hanging of Paul and Charles, who 'destroyed his innocence' when they took away his faith in man.

The long speech in which he explains the destruction of his innocence will be considered in some detail later. The essence of it is that he once believed in life and in humanity; he was in the position of a whole generation of humanists who, under the influence of such writers as Shaw and Wells, saw before them an inspiring prospect of human progress. Just as the Nazi extermination camps, the nuclear arms race and the outbursts of violence in Africa have made such optimism look silly, so in Procathren's personal life the shock of experience has shattered his beliefs. Life, which he had thought was an opportunity for men to do well by each other, now seems to him no more than a preparation for death. He says that Paul Southman has always known this, and Paul seems mutely to confirm this when he takes his hand. Procathren has arrived at the black pessimism that has since become familiar in literature. Melrose calls it fear of death, and Charles describes it as 'the corruption beneath the splendour, the maggot in the peacock.' But Procathren is no longer a peacock, and his attitude to death is no longer one of fear but of fascination. He had once feared the revelation by light of something beyond the darkness, but now he knows that there is nothing beyond the darkness but more darkness. Death is a kind of freedom. Sending Paul Southman and Charles Heberden to be hanged is no vindictive bloodthirstiness: death is what they have lived for, and he is fulfilling for them their destiny.

By healthy humanist standards Procathren's rejection of life will seem like the approach of madness. In his black despair, however, he has deepened as a character of the play and he has so matured in speech that we can now believe him to be a poet.

Charles Heberden is an artist of a kind that has become better understood since the emergence of the Beat movement. Beat poets and painters reject the values of modern society, withdraw from the scramble for success in terms of money and reputation, and concentrate on following their own artistic lights. (They need not be judged by their unwashed and untalented imitators who adopt beatnik attitudes as a fashionable pose.) Charles, after achieving fame at the age of fifteen, has turned his back on society and refuses to show his paintings. Procathren, the 'distinguished young poet and critic', stands for all that he despises most. Even before he has met him he guesses that he is 'clean, upright and bold ... full of a passionate desire for life. . . . He would say that he looks on life as an adventure and upon death as an enemy to be fought.' 'I once knew these beautiful poets,' he says. 'They smell. They smell very nice, but they smell.'

Charles really cares about painting. After Stella's death he has no compunction about using the corpse as a model so that he can get on with his mural.

His relations with Stella provide a poignant theme of the play. Marriage ought to mean accepting responsibility, being considerate, even tender; but Charles holds up to ridicule the man who is 'clean, temperate, respectable, responsible'. Yet in this painful love-hate relationship, it is not always Charles who is inadequate; Stella takes little interest in the pain that Charles suffers after his fall from the scaffolding. When Charles rightly disapproves of Stella's scheme to launch her aged grandfather on a new career, she utters malice born of her bitterness in words intended to hurt: 'You, with your paintings stored away unshown—probably unshowable—and your miserable fears of criticism! How dare you, a stranger . . .' This outburst is all the more painful when she immediately swings round to abject pleadings that she did not mean it. When opportunities arise for this unhappy pair to be drawn together, luck seems to be against them. There is the occasion when Charles discovers a white hair and unintentionally draws attention to the fact that Stella is much older than he is. Stella says, 'I'm ugly to you, aren't I, Charles?' He is here challenged to show some tenderness, but the old man breaks into the scene and the moment is lost. Later, when Stella makes a long and moving appeal for help in her loneliness, ending with the irresistible plea 'Oh Charles, Charles, comfort me!' he is about to move towards her when the trumpet sounds, bringing its disruptive menace from the outer world.

Charles is unlucky too in his attempts to be conventionally kind to the old man on his birthday. He hands him, a little awkwardly, a present. Before unpacking the scarf, Paul says, 'I hope it's not green. I don't like green things.' He takes out the scarf—and it is green. Such minor misfortunes are typical of the real difficulty of living together without hurting each other's feelings, a difficulty in the Southman household that is desperate for Stella.

But on the whole Charles gets on well with Paul. They understand each other and stimulate each other's mockery of the world they have renounced. They are theatrically exhilarating together. But Charles, like Paul, is destructive. He scorns the idea of life as an adventure, but he has not accepted it as an undertaking that can perhaps be shaped and made worth while.

If the catastrophe does not provoke in Charles the kind of transformation that we have seen in Paul and Procathren, it does nevertheless bring a moment of poignant self-revelation. We knew that he scorned success in society, the idea of life as an adventure; the world of responsibility and respectability; but we supposed that he believed in himself and his art. But when he curses Paul for taking refuge in lunacy he reveals a stark disillusion. He sees himself without pretence:

> If only I could convince myself, as you have done, that I am an artist, that the world waited to honour me, that the fires out there were a display for victory, that these brushes I hold were sceptres and these people princes. Then I might face the future.

Paul's comment is 'He's afraid—always has been'; but it sounds like a sort of courage. 'I can touch reality and know that I am nothing. . . .' At the end, when Paul deludes himself about where they are going, Charles indulges in no pretence.

Stella has womanly qualities that make her very different from her grandfather and her husband. She has a practical concern for material things, since she has to run the house and will have to bring up a baby; this becomes slightly repulsive at times, as when she says that the presentation cheque for Paul must come to her, even if it means that Procathren must contrive some trick. She is caught up in the feud with the villagers, but she has enough common sense to see how ridiculous is the military play-acting of 'General Southman and Captain Winter'. But the main difference is in her profound craving for emotional contact. For a young man it may be possible to meet a woman, offer her the flowers from his hat, move into the household and marry her, all without assuming responsibility, without offering her understanding or solicitude and without being deflected from his single-minded passion for painting: for a woman such detachment is unnatural. Stella sums up her state when she says: 'I am human and I am a woman.' Beside this simple assertion, considerations of whether she is a likeable or unlikeable character, whether she is more in the right than in the wrong, are irrelevant.

Her attitude to death is totally different from that of the men. She thinks of death as a state in which the memory of life on earth is all-important. Thus happy lovers build up 'a fabric of memory which will serve them well in their life after death when they will be together but alone.' This is apparently why happiness in life is important, and the prospect of 'all time being empty', a source of desperate fear.

The child Stella is an awkward, inarticulate substitute for the dead woman. Her importance to the play is as an object for Paul's new-found desire for human contact. He is not even sure whether she is a boy or a girl. At one moment he confuses her with his dead grand-daughter, when he says, 'O darling, darling Stella, it's a very great day for me, this birthday of mine.' If the child were pretty, charming and responsive, this scene might become cheaply sentimental.

Aldus is not a complicated character, but our reactions to him may be varying and contradictory. To Paul he is the ridiculous representative of the enemy, a holy bookworm, hardly worthy of his attention, but deserving to be humiliated and broken. The audience may enjoy the dramatic effectiveness of this scene, but at the same time sympathize with a man who appeals for help in his weakness, a man who is accustomed to acts dictated by reason, to law and order, and who is out of his depth when these values are repudiated. Stella has some sympathy, and is shocked by her grandfather's brutality towards the visitor. Later, Procathren also expresses contempt for Aldus, who amid the collapse of his world is 'still chasing his lost God like a rat down a culvert'. In the end he has been persuaded by Procathren that all his religious books are worthless. In his attempts to destroy them he burns down the whole village and is himself burnt to death in the church tower 'like a roasted potato'. There may here be an implied comment on the importance of the Church amidst the mass destruction and wholesale evil of the modern world; but the fact that the other men despise Aldus does not mean he is altogether despicable.

The soldiers offer a striking instance of the double level on which the play can be appreciated and understood. They are at once realistic and symbolic. On one plane their presence is fully explained and entirely credible in terms of everyday life, and one can imagine these absconders from a detention camp in every detail of their speech and behaviour: on the other plane they are the bringers of retribution, whose entrance is heralded by the strange, ominous notes of the trumpet. There is a harsh irony in the idea that they should be instruments of some sort of justice, for they are wholly destructive. And yet Melrose is the kind of instrument that Society finds useful for executing its more ruthless demands at home and overseas. He makes it quite clear that he will kill if somebody else takes the responsibility:

> If you want to order people like me around you've got to take the responsibility. . . . It makes me laugh sometimes, 'Melrose, do such and such!' 'Yes, sir.' And then I look down and see their eyes and their eyes are asking me, 'Melrose, you do think that decision is right, don't you? If you think I'm wrong for God's sake don't do it.' But I do it whatever I think—if I can be bothered to think.

Melrose says that he cares for nothing and explains that Procathren cannot understand him 'because he's lived in the world where people—well, where they behave. Where they do this or that for this or that reason—and they do this and that for this and that reason because they have a life to live—a life to plan—and they've got to be careful.' He will kill without reason if ordered to do so. So will his companions, but they are less analytical and less articulate.

As we have seen, they are not peculiar in this play in seeing no plan or reason in life; but they are appalling in their inhumanity. This is not to deny that they are fascinating characters on the stage.

John Winter represents a different example of obedience to orders. He is the loyal servant of Paul Southman, but when a different authority establishes itself he makes no protest, and at the end he gratefully and obsequiously accepts money from the murderers of his master. He is always addressed by his full name, and this indicates his position in the household: his Christian name alone would be too personal, his surname alone too distant. He is kept at a certain distance, and this he maintains.

The village women are common humanity caught up in disasters they do not understand. But they bear some share of responsibility, for when Thomas Cowper ran through the village streets nobody heeded him. 'The fire spread and nobody would help me—nobody came out—not even P.C. Pogson—until they were forced out by the fire.' John Whiting will not let us indulge in sentimental pity even for the dumb masses.

These, then, are the characters who came alive in the author's imagination to people that strange empty house in the Midlands, and some of them to take their places in the extraordinary painting on the wall. They are intensely alive, and the more the play is studied the more complete they are seen to be in detail. We come to know not only how Paul Southman came to this house twenty-five years ago, but how Stella grew up with her father and mother and sister. We are able to see more deeply into the personality of each character by studying his or her language—turns of phrase, rhythms, imagery—for speech is surely the chief means by which we reveal, betray, express, and sometimes try in vain to hide, our real selves.

Style

Good dialogue is the most important of theatrical qualities and the language of *Saint's Day* merits detailed study. It gives a genuine impression of naturalism, but the characters are more eloquent than real people; what they speak is more capable of pleasing the fastidious ear and stirring the imagination.

It is completely credible that Paul Southman should express himself by the full resources of educated language; he has been a great writer whose particular strength was in mockery;

moreover he has been 'a great one for acting' in his day. He is therefore in his element when mocking others or himself. Here is the experienced satirist describing Aldus—to his face:

> 'You will notice, my dears, first of all, the general attitude. That of humility bordering on servitude. It is dangerous to the unwary. It has been used by the Church for hundreds of years to gain advantage from a situation like this. Next, notice the facial expression. A cursory examination and one might take it to be shyness, perhaps idiocy. It is neither. . . . And the posture—neat, precise. If you were to go near him you would smell not sanctity but intrigue.'

He describes his own heyday in sardonic metaphor: 'Once I was a real Turtle. Then the world wasn't big enough for me to live in. Every time I raised my voice I banged my head.' He is at his most ebullient in the sustained metaphor by which he describes Society as a whore whom he exposed, and he is revelling in his own performance when he discovers that the expected visitor is already in the room.

The authority of his manner is reinforced by the formality of speech appropriate to his generation. He is usually acting a part. Thus he addresses John Winter as if he were a general directing military operations. This autocratic tone prepares us for the contrast when the broken old man at the end still retains some of the dignity of speech but without the spirit.

It is interesting to see that the habit of acting a part and using appropriate language has spread to John Winter, whose account of the situation in the village is praised by his master as 'an excellent and lucid report'.

> I can see no immediate danger to yourself, sir, from the situation at present. By their actions the soldiers have automatically allied themselves with us, although ignorant of our aims and even our existence. Indeed, by their actions they caused a diversion in the village admirably suited to the day of your visit to London.

Here the sentences are so consciously well-constructed, with a slightly old-world tone, that there is an element of parody.

Charles talks less than Paul. The staccato dialogue of the

opening of the play is typical. Later, when Stella pours out her unhappiness at great length, Charles answers briefly or not at all. Perhaps if he had talked more their relationship would not have become so sterile. At times his remarks have a laconic quality very characteristic of the younger generation of today. For instance, at the end of Procathren's careful explanation of what he is prepared to do for Stella, Charles comments: 'As an ally I prefer a dead dog.' When he speaks at greater length it is for purposes of derision, as in his forecast of what Procathren will be like: 'A fashionable man. His verse turned out as effortlessly as his personal appearance. Smooth thoughts soothing in their catholic simplicity.' He is the enemy of anything approaching cosiness, and his language is sharp and cold. But Paul and he indulge in bouts of mutual teasing or concerted movements of malicious fun at the expense of Stella and Procathren, and here the dialogue is a lively expression of the common ground between the old man and the youngster.

Stella is sharply contrasted with Charles in temperament and consequently in speech. She is deeply emotional, much preoccupied with her loneliness, her memories of childhood when her mother and her sister were alive, her frustrated longing for tenderness; and she tries to put all this into words. Genuinely naturalistic prose would be inadequate. The author succeeds in providing for her a language that generally sounds like ordinary speech, but is capable of taking on the tones of poetry when the emotion requires it. This poetic quality lies partly in the imagery (as when she says that lovers 'make a fabric of memory that will serve them well in their life after death'), but mainly in the sounds of the words and the rhythms of the sentences. Notice the melancholy cadences in the following passage, ending in the wistful memory of Charles's first appearance:

The family—my mother, my father and my sister—out there in the row of graves—what did they store up, I wonder? Dadda who fell from grace in the world when Paul fell, and spent the rest of his life living on the charity of the old man— what does he remember? Mamma—magnificent, angry Mamma—is she happy in the memory of her justice? Ellen, who died at twenty years, perhaps happy in the memory of my love for her. As for myself, if I die today, my eternal happiness will depend on the tiny memory of you, Charles—you, on your first visit to this place—standing in the door-way—(*she smiles*)—consciously picaresque—and handing me the flowers from your hat.

The poetic quality persists even when she speaks most simply, because the words beautifully carry the emotion: 'I am not a young girl. I am unused to laughter and my mind is always slow to understand. I can use neither wit not beauty. I can only appeal to his charity to take me away from this place. Perhaps I can go with him as his servant.'

There is one passage which is consciously reminiscent of T. S. Eliot both in matter and in tone:

Careful! We are approaching the point of deviation. At one moment there is laughter and conversation and a pro-gression; people move and speak smoothly and casually, their breathing is controlled and they know what they do. Then there occurs a call from another room, the realization that a member of the assembly is missing, the sudden shout into the dream and the waking to find the body with the failing heart lying in the corridor—with the twisted limbs at the foot of the stairs—the man hanging from the beam, or the child floating drowned in the garden pool. Careful! Be careful! We are approaching that point. The moment of the call from another room.

This passage is inspired by an uncanny moment of fore-knowledge; it describes the horror of the nightmare situation to come, when Stella is dead and Procathren shouts: 'Fools! You fools! Don't you understand? This is the shout from another room!' Such a foreboding could not be expressed except in terms of nightmare images. When it has passed Stella snaps back into the practical world to demand a cigarette. She has her practical, brisk moods when her language is as spare as Charles's, for her daily responsibilities demand a cool head and organizing ability.

When Procathren first arrives his language is flat and con-ventional. He makes a slightly pompous speech, which Paul spoils by interrupting to ask, 'What did he say?' He is embarrassed and out of his depth when Stella seeks to involve him in her troubles and Paul in his hostilities with the villagers. There is little energy at this time in his talk, but after the crisis he finds language to express his anguish. His long speech of explanation near the end is difficult to follow because the convulsion he describes is not rational and cannot be described in rational language. So he speaks in metaphors. Life, the opportunity to prepare for death, is his inheritance that he has wasted unaware. The dark is a familiar image of death, and one can imagine that seeing what lies beyond could be an awful revelation by light. Death revealing what is beyond is visualized as the unknown hand at the switch—a striking contemporary image. But now Procathren believes there is nothing beyond the darkness but more darkness, an image that attempts to describe nothingness.

It may be worth recalling the familiar passage in which Macbeth in a comparable state of mind expresses his conclusion that life is meaningless:

> All our yesterdays have lighted fools
> The way to dusty death. Out, out, brief candle!
> Life's but a walking shadow, a poor player,
> That struts and frets his hour upon the stage
> And then is heard no more; it is a tale
> Told by an idiot, full of sound and fury,
> Signifying nothing.

Like Procathren, he needs metaphor to utter what he feels.

When Procathren says that he ought to have realized that life was merely a preparation for nothingness, he refers to signs that he should have understood. Among these are 'the flowers in the sky, the sound of their blossoming too acute for our ears leaving us to hear nothing but the clamour of voices protesting, crying out against the end.' What are these strange, apocalyptic flowers? If they are atomic bombs whose invention and use may well shatter any faith in a purpose in human existence, why does not Procathren say so? Probably because the essence of his psychological or spiritual shock is that it is not to be rationally comprehended. Reduced to matter-of-fact words it would become manageable and commonplace. More-over, the author of the play is here only suggesting, without making it explicit, a link between the shock to Procathren of Stella's death and the shock to men generally of the events of the previous decade.

Another striking metaphor is that of mankind 'clinging to the walls of life in the storm that is of their own making, clamouring for tenderness, for love'. But Procathren sees no longer any salvation in compassion, or tenderness. Compassion, he says, is 'arid as an hour-glass' (not an object one associates with warm emotion). If the 'flowers in the sky' were marks of death for mankind, 'our own flowers' refers to the mark of blood where Stella was shot. Our last passport, which frees us from life, is blood. Blood is compared to the rose.[1] This is the imagery of poets who are half in love with death; here it half-persuades Procathren that he is offering a boon to Paul Southman.

The soldiers necessarily speak a less literary language than the rest. Melrose and his companions could easily appear among the soldiers in more recent plays like *The Long and the Short and the Tall,* though they do not use the contemporary army slang and cliché which gives such authentic flavour to the dialogue of such plays. This is soldier-talk for the more fastidious, but it sounds genuine enough, and conveys the right impression of men without ideals or illusions.

John Whiting's dialogue thus manages to reflect differences of character, generation and background, while retaining a consistent tone throughout the play. That tone is generally literary, but it succeeds admirably in communicating on two planes, the realistically commonplace and the poetically imaginative. At the time when *Saint's Day* was written the theatre appeared to be moving, under the leadership of T. S. Eliot and Christopher Fry, towards thorough-going poetic drama. John Whiting showed that prose that is naturalistic up to a point may still have the elegance and the emotional force of poetry.

[1] The rose is traditionally a symbol for the blood of a martyr.

Theatrical qualities

It is usual in these days to despise the so-called 'well-made play', in which the author exploits his characters and situations by efficient craftsmanship to make the maximum theatrical effect his prime objective. John Whiting is not a writer of well-made plays in this sense. Nevertheless, the theatrical qualities of *Saint's Day*, especially the first half, are outstanding. It is not surprising that it was the actors and directors, rather than the critics, who appreciated its virtues in 1951; it has acting parts that offer magnificent scope and a number of wonderfully exciting scenes for the stage. Among the latter are Procathren's arrival, the cross-examination of Aldus, and the similar treatment of Procathren which leads up to the tremendous climax of the shooting of Stella. It also has more quietly effective scenes, such as the opening, which establishes the atmosphere and explains the situation with great skill; haunting dramatic moments like the end of the first act when the trumpet is heard; and moving scenes like the last, in which there is the dramatic irony of Paul's calm concentration on preparations for what he says is the tree-felling and the audience knows is his execution. The sincerity and restraint here are qualities often lacking in the 'well-made play'.

It is worth noticing the skill with which physical objects necessary to the plot are introduced and used. For example, the trees on which Paul and Charles are hanged at the end are firmly established early in the play. In the first scene Stella wistfully recalls how she used to play in them as a child, but when Paul points out how withered, contorted and monstrous they have become she agrees that they should be cut down. We are told how they were in full leaf when the Southmans first came to the house twenty-five years before. After Stella's death Paul recalls how she was fond of them, but orders John Winter to get the tools so that they may cut them down. In the same way the copy of *Alice in Wonderland*, offered by Charles as an extra birthday present to Paul, acquires a recurring significance. Early in the play Paul reads out the beginning of the sorrowful Mock Turtle's story: 'Once I was a real Turtle,' and this

reminds him of the days when the world was not big enough
for him. He sums up in wry self-mockery the tragedy of his lost
greatness, of old age and declining powers; the note is echoed
ironically when he receives from Procathren the presentation
volume that is a tribute to what he once was; and it is all the
more poignant when he repeats it inconsequently in his
attempts to converse with the child Stella. The point is expressed again without words when the child picks up the book
as the last note of the trumpet tells us that the once-great turtle
is no more.

The pistol is another object that is firmly planted in the play.
It is mentioned jokingly as a source of danger before Paul first
comes in. Charles says: 'He's sitting on his bed cleaning a pistol.
You'd better be careful, John Winter.' But Winter laughs. Paul
brings it in when he threatens to avenge the supposed poisoning
of his dog; then he pretends to fire it at Aldus to frighten him;
finally in the fooling with Procathren it brings calamity. We
may connect the use of the pistol with the way in which nations
accumulate weapons and threaten to use them, only realizing
too late the risks involved; but it is not necessary to look for
symbolic importance in these objects: they are all understand-
able within the world of the Southmans.

The author skilfully ensures that we are familiar with the
trees, the book, or the pistol some time before they are to be
used at a crucial moment; and he extracts from each recurrence
an extra tang of meaning or emotion.

The most striking instance of this device is the treatment of
the trumpet. Like the soldiers who carry it, it can be thought of
on two planes, the realistic and the apocalyptic. The first time
it is heard it is mysteriously disturbing, and as the sound is
repeated the sense of foreboding grows, bringing the first act
to a dramatic conclusion. It is as haunting as the melancholy
sound of a string breaking in *The Cherry Orchard*, and as
ominous as the knocking in *Macbeth*. We later realize the
degree to which it is symbolic: it forebodes the fateful advent
of destructive forces from an outer world. But the trumpet is
next explained as a perfectly ordinary object: the absconding
soldiers have stolen it from among some band instruments that

were stored in the church hall. At the end it is both realistic and symbolic; its sound is a kind of Last Post blown by the soldiers to indicate to the audience that the execution has been carried out, and at the same time it recaptures the strange sense of foreboding with which we heard it first.

The play is full of other evidence of the mind of an experienced man of the theatre. If the dramatic force of its first two-thirds is not sustained in performance to the end, it is not because the construction loses grip: it is rather that there is too much matter. This 'density of texture', as John Whiting described it, makes full communication difficult in the theatre; but it rewards thorough reading of the text. Critics who expect a play to be fully understood at a first hearing must disapprove of many masterpieces. How many books have been written to explain what *Hamlet* is about? How much of the meaning of *King Lear* can be grasped without detailed study? *Saint's Day* remains exciting after many readings, and if at the end it leaves us asking questions, the play is in good company.

It must be admitted, however, that it does remain mysterious. Its atmosphere, which so strangely stirs the imagination, depends on our sense of wider importance and deeper meaning not wholly grasped. How much symbolic significance are we to read, for instance, into the elm trees, the dog, the irony of Melrose's Christian name, or poor Aldus roasting in his bell-tower? Soon one begins to suspect symbols at every turn. The author himself has warned us of the danger of over-investigation. 'The significance,' he said, 'is the total and overall effect.'

If a play makes sense in the theatre on the ordinary matter-of-fact level, nobody complains if it is also heavy with symbolism; but to appreciate *Saint's Day* one must be aware of more than the matter-of-fact. On the realistic plane, for example, Stella's description of the 'point of deviation' and the 'shout from the other room' seems no more than a theatrical device (not altogether appropriate to Stella) that will be fully exploited later; but if Stella is a kind of Cassandra prophesying calamity for the nations, the moment is a pregnant one. It is this sense of deeper meanings that gives its special quality to such a play as *Saint's Day*. The skilful craftsman who contrives a 'well-made play' makes sure of providing a dose that is easily assimilated: the true artist presents the vision that has inspired him, without himself analysing in detail what it means. The 'well-made play' makes its calculated effect in the theatre, and that is all; but plays like *Saint's Day* haunt the imagination much longer.

E. R. WOOD

SAINT'S DAY

CHARACTERS

STELLA HEBERDEN, *Paul's grand-daughter*

CHARLES HEBERDEN, *her husband*

PAUL SOUTHMAN, *an aged poet*

JOHN WINTER, *his manservant*

ROBERT PROCATHREN, *an admirer of Paul*

GILES ALDUS, *a recluse*

CHRISTIAN MELROSE
WALTER KILLEEN   } *three soldiers*
HENRY CHATER

HANNAH TREWIN
MARGARET BANT
EDITH TINSON
FLORA BALDON   } *people of the village*
JUDITH WARDEN
A CHILD
THOMAS COWPER

The play is in three acts, and the scene is laid in a room of Paul Southman's house in England on the twenty-fifth day of January.

ACT I.   Morning.
ACT II.   Early afternoon.
ACT III. Night.

Saint's Day was first produced at the Arts Theatre, London, on 5th September 1951. It was presented by The London Arts Theatre Committee Ltd., with the following cast:

PAUL SOUTHMAN	Michael Hordern
STELLA HEBERDEN	Valerie White
CHARLES HEBERDEN	Robert Urquhart
JOHN WINTER	Scott Harrold
ROBERT PROCATHREN	John Byron
THE REVEREND GILES ALDUS	Donald Pleasence
CHRISTIAN MELROSE	Ralph Michael
WALTER KILLEEN	Robert Mooney
HENRY CHATER	William Morum
THE CHILD	Peggy Palmer
JUDITH WARDEN	Anne Padwick
THOMAS COWPER	Bertram Shuttleworth
WOMEN OF THE VILLAGE	Judith Nelmes / Maureen Moore / Sabina Ward

The play directed by
STEPHEN MURRAY

Setting by Fanny Taylor.

ACT ONE

The day is the twenty-fifth of January : it is morning.

The scene is a room in Paul Southman's house. CHARLES *and* STELLA HEBERDEN *are present, motionless. The woman is standing by one of the three large central windows. The source of light behind the drawn curtains of the room is an oil-lamp carried by the man.*

STELLA: Listen!

> *They stand listening to the chimes of a distant church. The chimes end.*

CHARLES: Half-past.

STELLA: Nine?

CHARLES: Must be.

STELLA: Might be eight.

CHARLES: No.

STELLA: Surely not ten.

CHARLES: No, nine. Half-past nine. Is it raining now?

> STELLA *has moved to set the clock.*

STELLA: It might be any time, really. No, it's not raining now.

CHARLES: It was earlier this morning.   *He yawns.*

STELLA: The key's not on the ledge.

CHARLES: Look behind the clock. There?

STELLA: Yes. There wasn't——

CHARLES: It slips down. Can you get it?

STELLA: Yes. There wasn't any trouble in the night, was there?

CHARLES: No. (STELLA *begins to wind and set the clock.*) How long have you been up?

STELLA: Twenty minutes or so.

CHARLES: I didn't hear you.

STELLA: You were asleep. I shan't wind the strike.

CHARLES: No, don't. It's wrong, anyway. (*He calls.*) John Winter! John Winter! (*To* STELLA.) Where is he?

5

STELLA: I don't know. I haven't seen him this morning.

CHARLES: John Winter! (CHARLES, *wearing a woollen dressing-gown over his shirt—he is without trousers—stands on one leg, chafing a bare foot between his hands. He is below a narrow stairway, set within a wall, leading to an upper floor.*) I'm cold.

STELLA: Go and dress.

CHARLES: John Winter!

STELLA: If he could hear you he would've come by now.

CHARLES: He's up, I suppose.

STELLA: Now, Charles—don't shout again.

CHARLES: What?

STELLA: We don't want Paul to wake early. He's going to have a tiring day.

CHARLES: He's already awake. I heard him moving. (*He has opened the only door of the room and calls down the stairs to the kitchen, " John Winter ! "*) I heard him moving in his room as I came down. (*From his room above the narrow stairway* PAUL SOUTHMAN *calls, " John Winter ! ".*) There he is.

STELLA: Damn! I wanted him to sleep as late as possible this morning. Go up and——

CHARLES: Get John Winter to make a fire when he comes in.

STELLA: All right. Go up and try to persuade Paul to go back to bed for an hour.

CHARLES: He won't.

STELLA: Try to persuade him. I'm worried—— (PAUL SOUTHMAN *calls again: " John Winter ! "*) All right, Grandpa! (*To* CHARLES.) I'm worried as to whether the journey will tire him. I hope to God they don't give him anything to drink when he gets there. I'm sending John Winter with him—don't you think that's a good idea?

CHARLES: Yes. (*He is at the window drawing aside the curtains.*) It's going to be a fine day.

STELLA: Go up to him, will you, Charles. I don't want him to shout again or he'll start coughing.

CHARLES: All right. (*He takes up a man's bicycle which is lying in the centre of the room and props it against the wall.*) How are you this morning?

STELLA: All right now.

CHARLES: Sickness gone off?

STELLA: Yes. Yes, it goes when I've had a cup of tea and a biscuit.

CHARLES: Have you made some tea already?

STELLA: Yes.

CHARLES: Where is it?

STELLA: In our room. (CHARLES *goes towards the stairs.*) Didn't you see it?

CHARLES: No.

STELLA: Leave the lamp.

CHARLES: Sorry. (*As he goes up the stairs* PAUL SOUTHMAN *calls again : " John Winter ! "*) I'm coming.

PAUL: I want John Winter, not you. I want dressing.

> CHARLES *goes up the stairs.* STELLA *clears some dirty plates and cups from a central table and puts them on an ornate but filthy silver tray. She picks up a bicycle pump from the floor and fixes it into place on the bicycle. Going to the windows she draws back the curtains. The room is large : the building of the year* 1775. *There are three windows opening on to an iron balcony—entrance to the room can be gained by any of these windows. The balcony has iron steps leading down to the garden. There are two other entrances to the room : one, a door opening on to a small landing above stairs which lead to the kitchens and also to the main door of the house—two, a narrow stairway leading to the upper floors. This gives the room an elevation of being above the ground floor and yet below the main first floor. It stands alone, an architectural freak having no ceiling but a roof directly above it. There is an empty fireplace. The furnishing of the room is minimum for habitation : a table, and about it four chairs—two chairs and a low bench before the fireplace. The furnishings together with the various utilitarian objects about the room—the silver tray, the cups and dishes on the table—are of excellent quality but have lost their grace by neglect and misuse. Several hundred books are piled on the*

*floor in a corner of the room. From the right window
the wall of the room is curved and on the plaster surface
of the wall is an unfinished painting. This painting
represents five human figures and a dog—greater than
life-size—grouped about an, as yet, unspecified sixth
person. Executed in oils, it is harsh in texture, garish
in colour. Below the picture stands a small scaffolding
with painter's materials : there is also a ladder. The
floor of this part of the room before the painting is
raised six inches by means of a half-circular rostrum.*

The curtains withdrawn, STELLA *puts out the lamp. It is
light and promises to be a fine clear day.*

*The front door is heard to open and close ; footsteps sound
on the uncarpeted stairs from below.* JOHN WINTER
enters.

STELLA: Good morning, John Winter.

WINTER: Good morning, Miss Stella.

STELLA: You've been out already.

WINTER: Yes.

STELLA: Where?

WINTER: To get stuff for the fire.

STELLA: Surely you keep that in the cellar.

WINTER: You may remember——

STELLA: What? Speak up.

WINTER: I say you may remember I moved it some days ago.
I moved it from the cellar to my shed because of the damp
—it's mostly wood.

STELLA: I didn't know you'd moved it.

WINTER: Mr. Charles will remember. He helped me.

STELLA: Anyway, you've got the stuff for the fire.

WINTER: I've left it at the door. I didn't want to bring it in
until the room——

STELLA: Very well.

WINTER:—until the room had been tidied. I've already
cleaned the grate.

STELLA: You look frozen.

WINTER: It's very cold out of doors.

STELLA: Well, don't stand there! Grandpa—Mr. Southman

has been shouting for you. My husband has gone up to him.

WINTER: Should I light the fire first or go up and dress Mr. Southman?

STELLA: I don't know. I—— (*They stand silent for a moment.*) Oh, go and dress him but try to keep him in his room for a while. I want him to rest this morning. Just a minute! I want to talk to you. This man who is coming to visit us today——

WINTER: Mr. Procathren.

STELLA: You know about him?

WINTER: Mr. Southman mentioned him to me yesterday.

STELLA: You know today is Mr. Southman's birthday?

WINTER: Yes.

STELLA: In fact, you know all about it.

WINTER: That is all I know—that this gentleman is arriving on Mr. Southman's birthday. I think I should go up now.

He looks towards the stairs.

STELLA: Wait a minute! You may as well know it all. This Mr. Procathren—Robert Procathren—is a famous poet and critic. He is coming here to do honour to my grandfather on his birthday—honour as a poet. Late this afternoon Mr. Procathren, Mr. Southman and you will drive to London by car. You will go with them, do you understand? You will go with them to London.

WINTER: Yes.

STELLA: Those are the arrangements.

WINTER: Very well.

STELLA: There is to be a dinner in London tonight—Are you listening to me?

WINTER: Yes.

STELLA: You are not! Please pay attention. There is to be a dinner tonight in London in honour of Mr. Southman. It will be attended by very famous men and women. You will go with Mr. Southman. You won't go in to the dinner, of course, but wait outside. You will stay the night in London and be driven back tomorrow. Have you any better clothes than those?

WINTER: I have a blue suit.

STELLA: Wear it. One more thing—I shall cook the meal today. What food have we got? (WINTER *is silent*.) Have you any food at all in the house?

WINTER: There's some bacon and vegetables.

STELLA: We shall want some meat and something for—is there any fruit?—is there anything? And coffee—is there any coffee?

WINTER: No.

STELLA: Then you had better go down to the village this morning—early—and get these things. Do you understand?

WINTER: Yes.

STELLA: Go as soon as Mr. Southman has finished with you.

WINTER: I shall need money.

STELLA: Here you are. (*She takes a ten-shilling note from her pocket and gives it to* JOHN WINTER.) That's all right, then? (JOHN WINTER *does not reply*.) Don't be so sullen, John Winter! You may be the servant but you know the position as to money as well as I do. We cannot pay those bills in the village at present—but we will in time. Promise them that. You can tell them—promise them— you—because they respect you down in the village—yes, they respect you.

WINTER: They hate me.

STELLA: Nonsense.

WINTER: Truth.

STELLA: Hate you?

WINTER: Of course—why not?—despise me—hate me, they do. I say, why not? A beggar—I have to go to them— a little food—say, a little meat—a little bread—later— a little more bread—a little more meat—Please!

STELLA: John Winter!

WINTER: One day they'll stop—or I'll stop—and then what will happen?

STELLA: Are you threatening me? (*He is silent*.) I say, are you threatening me? (*He shakes his head*.) Come now, you wouldn't like to see Mr. Southman or his guest go without food, would you? Would you? No, of course, you wouldn't, because you love him as I love him, and we'll fight for him, won't we? We'll put our pride in our pocket and we'll fight for him. We've got to look after him, you know. There's no one else. Just you and me, that's all. Now, go along. (CHARLES *comes down the stairs : he is dressed and carries a cup of tea.*) John Winter. (STELLA *goes to* JOHN WINTER *and puts her arms about him.*) John Winter, I want you to go with my grandfather today—go with him to London—because I trust you. Remember, he will be among strangers—all his friends have gone—and he may be frightened. And if he is afraid he will appear ridiculous. I want you to see that he is not frightened—that by his age he is great and not ridiculous. That he is Paul Southman.

WINTER: He is a great and famous man.

STELLA: Of course he is. And today we have an opportunity to remind the world of that. Now, go up and get him dressed, but try to keep him in his room.

WINTER: I've put out his best clothes.

STELLA: He's waiting for you.

CHARLES: He's sitting on his bed cleaning a pistol. You'd better be careful, John Winter.

JOHN WINTER *laughs and goes up the stairs.*

STELLA: I told you I'm sending John Winter up to London with Paul, didn't I?

CHARLES: Yes. Are you going to light a fire?

STELLA: Later.

CHARLES: I'm so cold.

STELLA *fetches an oil-stove from a corner of the room. She lights it.*

STELLA: Sit over this.

CHARLES: Look! *He points to the ornate pediment over the door.*

STELLA: What?

CHARLES: There's a bird—above the door. It's hiding there—behind the scroll.

STELLA: They fly in sometimes. They don't come to any harm.

CHARLES: What was all that just now?

STELLA: When?

CHARLES: With John Winter.

STELLA: Oh, a minor revolt—over getting food from the village. He says they hate him down there. I suppose it's true. They hate us all. Is that stove alight?

CHARLES: Yes.

STELLA: They hate us because they don't understand our isolation. They don't understand us and so they fear us. They fear us and so they hate us.

CHARLES: But only passively. They——

STELLA: Not at all. Do you know that three years ago— before you came here—there was a plan among the villagers to attack this house. Everything was arranged, but on the decided night they sat drinking to get up their courage and when the time came they were all too drunk to walk the half-mile to the house. So the attack didn't come off that time. It may some day.

CHARLES: What would they do?

STELLA: Paul says they'd kill us.

CHARLES: It must be hard for John Winter. He has to go down among them—we don't.

STELLA: Well, I've given him some money this morning so he'll be all right.

CHARLES: By the way, I've got this. (*He takes some coins from his pocket.*) You'd better have it.

STELLA: Thank you.

CHARLES: Do you think John Winter could do something for me in London?

STELLA: What?

CHARLES: If he has time.

STELLA: Well, what?

CHARLES: I've got a small canvas I think I can sell—might get ten pounds for it—if John Winter could take it round to the dealers for me tomorrow.

STELLA: Charles! Will you? Will you really try to sell it? Ten pounds would help so much.

CHARLES: It's that small oil I did of you three months ago. You don't want it?

STELLA: If you sell it we shall be able to——

CHARLES: You don't want it?

STELLA: No, I don't want it. We shall be able to——

CHARLES: Very well! (*A pause.*) Then that's settled.

STELLA: Yes. I'll tell John Winter. (STELLA *moves to* CHARLES.) I'm sorry, Charles, but we must have money.
CHARLES *moves away from her.*

CHARLES: I know.

STELLA: If only Grandpa would begin to write again. Anything! I'm sure they'd take it. Take it on his name alone. People haven't forgotten him.

CHARLES: Of course they have.

STELLA: They haven't! If they've forgotten him why should this man Procathren be coming down today to take him to London?

CHARLES: The whole thing is probably a stunt. Listen, Stella. Who is going to be at that dinner tonight? I'll tell you. Fashionable people. Poets, painters, novelists and critics à la mode. The kind of people who, twenty-five years ago when Paul wrote his pamphlet " The Abolition of Printing ", turned against him and drove him into this exile and silence. Those are the people who will be receiving him, applauding him tonight. (*There is a pause.*) I don't think you understand, Stella. We've had all this so often before. Why can't you leave the old man alone? For him to attempt to begin again—No, I don't think you could understand.

STELLA: Of course I understand.

CHARLES: Let me put it this way. Go to London today and ask a hundred people who know of Paul—ask them about him—and ninety-nine of them will say he died years ago. I tell you even those who haven't forgotten him think he's dead. His name in a newspaper tomorrow would cause nothing but surprise. Let the few eminent people who do remember him enjoy the entertainment tonight. It won't do them or Paul any harm, but don't you build anything from it—useless and unkind.

STELLA: Charles, this is a chance we've never had before. He'll be remembered by this dinner. Now is the time for him to start writing again. We needn't bother about the physical effect on him—I can do the writing if he'll dictate. Anything! Articles, satires—any of the things that made him famous—made him Paul Southman, the pamphleteer and lampoonist, the poet and revolutionary.

CHARLES: He's eighty-three.

STELLA: I know.

CHARLES: All those things—useless—he's an old man—quite out of touch—he has no idea what has happened in the outside world in the last twenty-five years. There have been changes, you know.

STELLA: Then we'll start taking the newspapers again. I'll try to get him out, even if it's only to the village. We'll buy some new books and I'll read to him.

CHARLES: You know he can't concentrate for two minutes either reading or being read to. You know he will never go to the village. You know—you must know he's a very old man and he's finished. Finished! I'm trying to explain in such a way that you can understand. (*Pause.*) It won't work, Stella. (*Pause.*) Let him die in peace. (*Pause.*) Let him alone.

CHARLES *goes to the door.*

STELLA: Charles, I want to speak to you. Charles! (*He stops at the door.*) I've lied to you.

CHARLES: What?

STELLA: I've lied to you.

CHARLES: What about this time? (*She does not answer.*) Come along, you know you enjoy the confession more than the lie. I suppose you're not going to have a child.

STELLA: No, it's not that. I've lied to you about my age.

CHARLES: Well?

STELLA: I told you I was twenty-eight last birthday. I was really thirty-two.

CHARLES: That makes you twelve years older than me instead of eight. All right.

STELLA: I don't——

CHARLES: Did you think four years would make so much difference?

STELLA: You look so young.

CHARLES: And who is there to see me but you?

STELLA: This morning there will be Robert Procathren. I was going to suggest that we pretend to him that you're my brother—not my husband.

CHARLES: Don't be absurd!

STELLA: Is it absurd? Well, never mind. Go and get yourself some breakfast.

CHARLES: Yes, I will. And Stella——

STELLA: Yes?

CHARLES: Don't try to get the old man back to work.

STELLA: All right. But I think it would be a good thing—not only for us, but for him.

CHARLES (*in sudden anger*): It would not! It would not be a good thing. It would not be a good thing for any of us. What is it you're hankering after? You want something from it. You're planning something, aren't you—aren't you?

STELLA: Don't speak to me like that!

> *In silence* STELLA *picks up the tray and goes out of the room and down the stairs to the kitchens below.* CHARLES *shouts after her.*

CHARLES: It's only that you don't understand. (*He is unanswered. He goes to the stove and warms his hands : he ties his shoe-laces : he goes to the scaffolding set below the mural painting : he examines the painter's materials set on the scaffolding.* STELLA *returns to the room. She begins to wipe the table with a damp cloth.* CHARLES *speaks.*) I've got a pain in my side. (*A pause.*) Had it last night. Worse this morning. (STELLA *does not reply.*) Here. (*He indicates the position of the pain.* STELLA *ignores this and* CHARLES *turns back to the painter's material.*) Do you think John Winter could get me some stuff in London?

STELLA: I should think so.

CHARLES: Now, what do I want? I want some——

STELLA: Write it down.

CHARLES: What time is this fellow arriving?

STELLA: No special time. Just this morning.

CHARLES: Procathren—Procathren.

STELLA: What do you say?

CHARLES: Nothing. Have you got Paul anything for his birthday?

STELLA: Yes. A pair of slippers.

CHARLES: Where are they?

STELLA: In the table drawer. Why?

CHARLES: When are you going to give them to him?

STELLA: When he comes down, I suppose.

> CHARLES *has taken a small parcel from the canvas bag hanging on the scaffolding.*

CHARLES: Will you give him this at the same time?

STELLA: Why don't you give it to him yourself?

CHARLES: No, you. Here you are. It's a scarf—woollen scarf. Take it.

> STELLA *takes the parcel and puts it in the table drawer.*

STELLA: Where's the pain?

CHARLES: What?

STELLA: The pain you said you had—where is it?

CHARLES: Here.   STELLA *puts her hand to his side.*

STELLA: Bad?

CHARLES: Rather. I may have strained myself. I fell from there—(*He indicates the scaffolding.*)—yesterday. I called out for you as I fell—you didn't hear me. Just a minute. You've got a cobweb in your hair. Stand still. (*His hands go to her head.*) No. No, it's your hair. White. Your hair is——

PAUL: They must go. I have decided—(PAUL SOUTHMAN *can be heard speaking to* JOHN WINTER *as they come down the stairs.*)—we could manage it between us——

CHARLES: Your hair is going white.

PAUL: You think I'm too old, but I could give you a hand.

STELLA: Charles!

PAUL: Away with them. That's what I say—careful!— then we shall have a clear view——

STELLA: Charles!

PAUL: —a clear view if anything threatens.

STELLA: I'm ugly to you, aren't I, Charles?

PAUL (*laughing*): What do I mean by that, eh, John Winter?

STELLA: Charles! Speak to me. I'm ugly to you, aren't I?

PAUL: As it threatens at all times we must be prepared. (PAUL SOUTHMAN *and* JOHN WINTER *reach the foot of the stairs*.) Good morning.

STELLA: Good morning, Grandpa.

CHARLES: Good morning, Paul.

PAUL: What's the time?

STELLA: About a quarter to ten.

> JOHN WINTER *puts a chair beside the oil-stove*. PAUL *sits*.

PAUL: Thank you. I've just been telling John Winter about an idea of mine. A precaution. I'll tell you later. I'll have some breakfast now, John Winter. (JOHN WINTER *goes out*.) Is there no fire?

STELLA: We'll have one lit in a few minutes.

PAUL: Good. It's very cold. I've been very cold in bed all night. (*He looks up at* STELLA *and* CHARLES, *smiling*.) It is today I have to play the great man, isn't it?

STELLA: Yes.

PAUL: You notice I'm dressed up?

STELLA: You look very nice.

PAUL: You understand I realise the importance of today?

STELLA: I hope you do.

PAUL: Is the weather going to be fine?

STELLA: I think so.

PAUL: The sun shining?

STELLA: I hope so.

PAUL: The flags hung out in London for me?

STELLA (*laughing*): Perhaps.

PAUL (*laughing*): Excellent.

STELLA: Many happy returns of the day, Grandpa.

> *She gives him her present*.

PAUL: God bless my soul!

STELLA: God bless you, indeed—pretending you didn't expect it.

PAUL: How neatly it's parcelled up—with such a tight little

knot. What is it, I wonder? I am supposed to be able to open it, am I? I mean, there is something inside.

STELLA: Let me do it.

PAUL: No, no. I've done it now. (*He has undone the parcel and holds up the pair of slippers.*) For my feet?

STELLA: And this is from Charles.

> CHARLES *turns away.*

PAUL: What is it, Charles?

> JOHN WINTER *enters carrying a cup of tea and a plate of rusks.*

CHARLES: A scarf.

STELLA: You musn't tell him.

CHARLES: Knitted by myself with wool from a pair of my old socks.

PAUL: Excellent! Now I shall be warm at both ends. (*He pauses in undoing the parcel.*) I hope it's not green. I don't like green things. (*He takes out the scarf : it is green.*)

STELLA: Put it on, Grandpa. You look very-handsome. Doesn't he, Charles?

PAUL: Do I?

STELLA: Of course you do, darling.

> JOHN WINTER *takes a box of cigarettes from his pocket. He holds it out to* PAUL.

PAUL: What's this?

WINTER: Birthday present, sir.

PAUL: Thank you, John Winter. I forgot your last birthday, didn't I?

WINTER: Yes, sir.

PAUL: Good of you to remember mine. Cigarettes. Have one?

WINTER: Thank you.

STELLA: Now, Grandpa, you don't want to smoke. Have your breakfast first.

PAUL: Very well. (*He begins to dip the rusks in the tea.*) Stella, John Winter and I have been discussing—Stella!

STELLA: Yes?

> *She has been whispering with* CHARLES *who begins to go from the room.*

PAUL: John Winter and I have been—Where's Charles going?

CHARLES: I'm going to get some breakfast. Can I pinch one of your cigarettes?

> *After* CHARLES *has taken a cigarette* PAUL *puts the box into his pocket.* CHARLES *goes out.*

PAUL: John Winter. John Winter where are you?

WINTER: Here.

PAUL: I saw the dog from my window just before I came down. He was limping. What's the matter with him? You haven't been beating him again, have you?

WINTER: I never beat him.

PAUL: I've told you before—I won't have that dog beaten. Do you understand?

WINTER: Yes.

PAUL: He may misbehave himself but he's getting old and he doesn't know what he's doing. He's getting old and a little simple. I suppose you'll be beating me soon. Now remember——

STELLA (*to* JOHN WINTER): You'd better get down to the village. I want those things.

PAUL: Is John Winter going out?

STELLA: Yes. He's going down to the village to get some food. We can't give Mr. Procathren bacon.

PAUL: Why not?

STELLA: Go along, John Winter. Meat, bread, dried fruit of some kind and coffee.

> JOHN WINTER *begins to wheel the bicycle from the room.* PAUL *calls after him.*

PAUL: O, brave John Winter! Going down among the enemy again. Would you like to take my pistol? Be careful not to break wind in the High Street or they'll be after you. (JOHN WINTER *has left the room.*) One day they will.

STELLA: What?

PAUL: Kill him.

STELLA: No.

PAUL: Why not?

STELLA: Like them, he's a servant; they would never kill one of their own kind. They hate him, perhaps, but——

PAUL: Are you suggesting that John Winter is working with the villagers against us?

STELLA: No, of course not.

PAUL: Such a thing had never occurred to me. Is it likely?

STELLA: No.

PAUL: Is it?

STELLA: No! Don't get such an idea into your head. I didn't mean to suggest it. John Winter is loyal. He loves you dearly.

PAUL: He beats the dog.

STELLA: He denies that.

PAUL: I won't have that dog beaten. I must exert my authority. John Winter is my servant, and he shall obey my orders.

STELLA: Of course. (*A pause.*) What are you thinking?

PAUL: He moves quite freely among the villagers, you know.

STELLA: To spy on them. So that we can be warned of any danger. Now come, Grandpa. Don't be silly. Of course John Winter is loyal to us. Remember the night when they intended to attack the house and John Winter sat with you out there on the balcony waiting for them. He was prepared to fight with you against them—against his own kind. Remember that. (PAUL *is silent.*) What was it you were telling him before you came down?

PAUL: It is absurd òf me to doubt him. Absurd! It was cold that night, you know, but he didn't complain. No, he made jokes—very good jokes too—about the villagers. He's brave and he's loyal. It is ridiculous to doubt his honesty.

STELLA: Of course it is ridiculous. What were you telling him as you came down? I'm interested.

PAUL: What? Oh, yes. Yes, Stella. You know the two trees, the elms—that stand in front of the house——?

STELLA: Tweedledum and Tweedledee—yes?

PAUL: What's that?

STELLA: We used to call them that when I was a child—don't

you remember? (*She puts her hands in a defensive boxing attitude.*) Their arms outstretched in constant conflict—remember?

PAUL: Yes, of course. They're dead now.

STELLA: Yes, they're dead now.

PAUL: And I'm going to cut them down.

STELLA: Why?

PAUL: Because they are a danger.

STELLA: To whom?

PAUL: To ourselves. I saw them yesterday as they are—blanched by age—withered, contorted and monstrous. They shouldn't stand before the house. They must be brought down.

STELLA: I played in them when I was a child—with Ellen.

PAUL: You agree they should come down?

STELLA: If you think it's necessary.

PAUL: I believe it is necessary. And it must be done quickly.

STELLA: Very well.

PAUL: That way it will give us less pain. I remember them, too. They were in full leaf the summer morning I arrived here twenty-five years ago. On approach they quite obscured the house and when you were before the door they shadowed you. But now they're dead and must be brought down. I can do it with John Winter.

STELLA: You mustn't do it! Not yourself.

PAUL: With John Winter. You don't think I'm strong enough? I'm quite strong enough. It will have to be carefully done for they must fall away from the house. (*He takes the cigarettes from his pocket.*) I think I might have a cigarette now.

STELLA: Yes.

PAUL: Nice of John Winter. Look! He's written on the box. What does it say?

STELLA (*She reads*): "Many happy returns of the day. Your obedient servant, John Winter."   *They laugh.*

PAUL: Absurd of me to suspect him of treachery.

STELLA: Absurd.

PAUL: Have one?

STELLA: Thank you, I will.

PAUL: I suppose John Winter stole them.

STELLA: I suppose so.

PAUL: Sit down.

STELLA: I have a lot to do.

PAUL: For a few minutes. Whilst we smoke our cigarettes. (STELLA *pulls up a stool and sits by him.*) Have you matches?

STELLA: Yes.

PAUL: You remember the trees from your childhood— Tweedledum and Tweedledee?

STELLA: Yes. Is that foolish?

PAUL: I don't think so.

STELLA: Somehow I—Tell me, are they evil now?

PAUL: Not evil—dangerous.

STELLA: They were most benevolent to Ellen and me when we were children. They were almost our only playthings and gave themselves so willingly to masquerading as other places—other worlds.

PAUL: But they're ugly now—ugly and old and dead.

STELLA: Yes.

PAUL: So I shall cut them down.

STELLA: Very well. When did they die?

> CHARLES, *below in the kitchen, shouts :* Get out! Get out!

PAUL: What? What's that? What?

STELLA: Charles. (*She goes to the door and calls down the stairs.*) Charles!

CHARLES (*from below*): All right. It's the dog.

STELLA: It's the dog.

PAUL: Well, what's he doing to it?

STELLA: I don't know.

PAUL: Why do you all hate that dog so much?

STELLA: We don't.

PAUL: You never seem to give him a moment's peace.

STELLA: He's so large and he will come into the house—and he's begun to smell terribly.

PAUL: Probably I do. I'm getting old. I suppose I shan't be allowed in the house soon.

STELLA: Don't pity yourself.

PAUL: What did you say?

STELLA: Nothing.

PAUL: Stella! What did you say?

STELLA: Charles is really very good to him.

PAUL: Then why does he shout at him? And look—look! What's he doing here? (*They turn to look at the painting.*) What does it mean? What are those monstrous figures? And there's the dog—see? At least I suppose it's my dog. I don't understand such things.

STELLA: He'll say very little about it.

PAUL: Has it a title?

STELLA: I don't know.

PAUL: Things should always be titled. Does he tell you nothing?

STELLA: Very little.

PAUL: I don't understand him. I was nearly sixty when I gave up my work and came to live here—and there was a reason. I was victimised—driven here by my enemies. Charles's work as a painter was recognised when he was —how old?

STELLA: Fifteen.

PAUL: And now he's twenty. There was no attack on him, or on his work. He was acclaimed as a prodigy. Yet he came here, met you, married you—strange, you—and now lives with the old fellow—the poor man. Refuses to show his paintings—except that. What is to go there?

> *He indicates the unfinished lower part of the mural.*

STELLA: There? Oh, another figure—a woman. Charles wants me to model for it but I haven't had time as yet.

PAUL: A woman. Then the other figures—those—will be looking down at her, eh?

STELLA: I suppose so.

PAUL: I don't understand it.

STELLA: Don't——

PAUL: I don't understand it at all.

STELLA: Don't let it worry you. Leave him in peace.

PAUL: Charles? I will. But he musn't harm the dog. Is that clock right?

STELLA: I think so. I put it right by the village.

PAUL: Procathren should——

STELLA: Oh, Grandpa! (*She laughs.*) I've got something to show you. I found it last night. (*She has taken a page of a magazine from the pocket of her dress and unfolded it.*) It's from a magazine called "The Tatler"—an old copy— some years ago—look——

PAUL: Who is it?

STELLA: Read it.

PAUL (*puts on his spectacles and reads*): "The Honourable Robert Procathren, distinguished young poet and critic, photographed last week after his marriage to Miss Amanda Mantess, daughter of Mr. and Mrs. Sebastian Mantess of——" it's torn away. What a beautiful young man!

STELLA: Isn't he?

PAUL: Fancy such an elegant and obviously witty person coming to see us.

STELLA: Why not?

PAUL: But, I mean, look at him. Look at his clothes. His hair is trimmed and I'm sure, if you could see them, his finger-nails would be spotless. His linen is as crisp as the paper on which he has been writing to me. Oh, dear! He's obviously very famous and very correct. What on earth shall I say to him? Look at those dainty feet in the pointed shoes. (*He stamps in his great black boots.*)

STELLA: Are you making fun of him?

PAUL: Indeed, no. He frightens me.

STELLA: What do you mean?

PAUL: Come, child, you know what is meant by fear. I'm afraid of him——

STELLA: Paul!

PAUL:—his whole appearance is alien to me.

STELLA: His appearance. But, my dear, appearance has never counted with you. Do you mean his clothes? It doesn't matter what he wears, but what he is as a man.

PAUL: About tonight, Stella——

STELLA: He is your admirer—he is coming here to express that admiration. And you can meet him—I give you my word—not as an equal but as his superior. You see—he'll admit that.

PAUL: How you do talk. But, darling, I'm frightened about tonight.

STELLA: You musn't be.

PAUL: Why don't you try to understand?

STELLA: You musn't be frightened.

PAUL: I——

STELLA: Look at me. Do you love me?

PAUL: I do.

STELLA: Then if you love me you won't be frightened.

PAUL: So simple? I'm old. Easily frightened.

STELLA: Paul—Paul!

She grasps his arm.

PAUL: You're hurting me.

STELLA: You are greater than any of them. They understand that by these last twenty-five years of exile and mortification you have proved the justice and truth of those opinions expressed in your pamphlets. You have proved your integrity and saintliness and tonight it is that that they will honour. Paul! You're not going before a tribunal.

PAUL: Ha! They will be in judgement on my table manners.

STELLA: It is your poetry they will be remembering.

PAUL: They'll laugh at my fumbling with the knives and forks.

STELLA: They will remember your political writings.

PAUL: A stupid old man! I shan't be able to eat the food they give me. A glass of wine goes to my head and makes me babble like a baby. I shall want to go to the lavatory during their speeches and I shan't be able to go. I shall wet myself again and then you'll be angry with me. O Stella!

There is a pause—then STELLA *speaks with gentleness.*

STELLA: There is nothing to fear. I promise you that. I've never promised you anything that has not been perfectly fulfilled, have I? Have I?

PAUL: No.

STELLA: Then you can trust in this promise. You will not be afraid today. (*She gives him her handkerchief.*) Dry your tears.

PAUL: I feel giddy.

STELLA: It's the cigarette. Do you remember what you said when you came downstairs this morning?

PAUL: Within twelve hours——

STELLA: Do you remember what you said? " It is today I have to play the great man, isn't it? " That's what you said.

PAUL: I was joking, dear Stella.

STELLA: Joking or not—that is what you must do. Play the great man. Now, at this moment, you may tell me of your fears. At this moment, because we are alone and I love you. But from the time of Procathren's coming here you must act the great man. You must meet this elegant and witty young man with your own elegance and wit. Good gracious me! From what Mamma told me you were a great one for acting in your day. (PAUL *laughs.*) Were you? Then remember that when you meet these people.

PAUL: I wish I had some better clothes.

STELLA: You look very well as you are.

PAUL: Newer clothes.

STELLA: And Grandpa——

PAUL: Yes?

STELLA: Also remember—this is a new beginning for you. For twenty-five years—since I was a child, we have been waiting for this moment. Don't fail! Don't fail, now! Go to London today, meet these people, show them that you are yet alive and active and then—then begin to write again. Do this and you won't have to act the great man—you will be the great man.

There is a pause.

PAUL: And what do you hope to get out of all this, Stella?

> CHARLES *comes into the room from below.*

STELLA: Nothing—I swear it! Nothing—I believe in you!

PAUL: Take this cigarette from me.

STELLA: Perhaps they have asked you to return because they need you. Perhaps they are in trouble out there and want your wisdom, your advice. Have you thought of that?

PAUL: Why should I give them my advice? They are nothing to me.

CHARLES: Bravo!

PAUL: Hullo, Charles.

STELLA: It is your duty, Grandpa.

CHARLES: Nonsense!

STELLA (*she turns to* CHARLES): You, my precious little fellow —and what do you know about it?—you being a stranger here. You, with your paintings stored away unshown— probably unshowable—and your miserable fears of criticism. Well, Paul, does not need to fear criticism. He can go out from here into the world—unafraid—disarming criticism and censure by his genius. Then how dare you, a stranger——

CHARLES (*shouting*): Stella!

> *There is a pause.*

STELLA: Yes, Charles?

CHARLES: I want to speak to you.

> *He goes up the stairs.*

STELLA: Yes, Charles.

> *She follows him up the stairs.* PAUL *left alone, stares at the newspaper cutting in his hand. From the head of the stairs the voices of* CHARLES *and* STELLA *rise together.*

CHARLES: —damnable, damnable things!——

STELLA: —unmeant, unmeant——

CHARLES: —cruel wickedness, most cruel!——

STELLA: —not meant. I never mean to—never mean to——

> PAUL, *staring at the newspaper cutting, suddenly cries out.*

PAUL: O God! O God!

> *There is silence—then* STELLA *calls.*

STELLA: What is it, Grandpa? (*She comes down the stairs.*) What is it?

> PAUL *holds up the newspaper cutting.*

PAUL: Stella—Stella, look at this man.

> CHARLES *comes down the stairs.*

STELLA: I've seen it, Grandpa. Your nose is running. Wipe it.

CHARLES: Has John Winter gone out?

STELLA: Yes.

CHARLES: I thought he was going to light the fire before he went.

STELLA: It's more important that we should have the food.

CHARLES: I'm so damned cold. Move over, Paul, and let me have a bit of the stove.

PAUL: Charles. I say, Charles, look at this.

> He holds out the cutting.

CHARLES: Just a minute. Stella—(*She is combing her hair before a fragment of glass set on the mantelpiece.*)—when will you have time for me to start work on that last figure?

STELLA: I don't know.

PAUL: Charles, look!

CHARLES: Just a moment, Paul. Do you think today, Stella?

STELLA: No, not today. I shan't have a minute to sit today.

CHARLES: Why not, when Paul's gone?

STELLA: Well, I'll see, but I don't know.

CHARLES: I've been asking you for the last three weeks.

STELLA: I know.

CHARLES: Now then—what do you want, Paul?

PAUL: Look at this.   CHARLES *takes the cutting.*

CHARLES: Who is it?

PAUL: Read it.

CHARLES (*He reads*): "The Honourable Robert Procathren, distinguished young——" Oh!

PAUL: Isn't he a grand young fellow?

CHARLES: Indeed, he is. Stella, have you seen this?

STELLA: I gave it to Paul.

CHARLES: Where did you find it?

STELLA: Among some old magazines of yours.

PAUL: Look! Look, Charles, what do they say?

CHARLES: "—distinguished young poet and critic——"

PAUL: "—distinguished young poet and critic——"

CHARLES (*He nudges* PAUL): Paul, my old one——

PAUL (*giggling with anticipation*): Yes? Yes, sonny, yes?

CHARLES: A splendid young man. Isn't he, Stella? Paul—Paul, tell me——

PAUL: Yes, sonny? Yes, what?

CHARLES: Isn't he the kind of young man Stella admires—very much admires? Clean, upright, bold——

PAUL: Yes? Yes?

CHARLES:—full of a passionate desire—for life. Not like us, my ancient—not like you and me—being, as we are, despised by Stella. No, she'd admire him—this Procathren.

STELLA (*She turns and shouts*): I'm not going to quarrel with you!

CHARLES: —admire him very much for what he is and for what he does—the conduct of his life. Yes, Stella would love him—love him dearly——

STELLA: Damn you, Charles! Damn you!

CHARLES: And what is he, Paul, this Procathren?

PAUL: Tell me—tell me!

CHARLES: He is a man. And being a man may we conjecture what he would say to a woman like Stella? I think we may.

PAUL: Yes, I think we may.

CHARLES: He would say that he looks upon life as an adventure, and upon death as an enemy to be fought with desperation. Age as something to be accepted with dignity—women also. A man lacking in pathos but not lacking in attraction. Therefore, a man clean, temperate, respectable, responsible——

STELLA: I shall leave the room!

CHARLES: —restrained, realistic, reasonable——

PAUL: A lovely man!

CHARLES: A fashionable man. His verse turned out as effortlessly as his personal appearance. Smooth thoughts soothing in their catholic simplicity. Love poems—ah, Stella!—a delicious liquidity—casually inspired by the contemplation of his elegant mistress's inner thighs. Not like your—(*He nudges* PAUL *who giggles.*)—not like your blasphemous, bawdy, scraggy limericks. Yes, Stella, I once knew these beautiful poets. They smell. They smell very nice, but they smell.

STELLA: You're jealous.

CHARLES: Yes, my love.

STELLA: You! You lack attraction but, my God! you don't lack pathos. As you are now—as you are sitting there now—I could weep for you——

CHARLES: There's someone——

STELLA: Weep for you!

CHARLES: There's someone on the stairs.

> *Footsteps can be heard coming up the stairs from below.*

STELLA: Listen!

CHARLES: It's probably him. (*To* PAUL.) Here he comes to take you away.

STELLA: Behave yourselves! Are you ready?

CHARLES: Ready. (CHARLES *rises, and, standing behind* PAUL, *whispers.*) Your flies are undone.

> PAUL *looks, finds they are not undone, and laughs.*

STELLA: Be quiet!

> *She is about to move to the door when it is opened from the outside and* JOHN WINTER *comes into the room. He is carrying parcels of food.* CHARLES *and* PAUL *shout with laughter.*

CHARLES: The distinguished critic!

PAUL: Do I bow, or curtsey, or salute, or——

> *Laughing, he proceeds to do all these things.*

STELLA: You make me look a fool, John Winter.

WINTER: I'm sorry.

CHARLES: Blame me, Stella. Blame me.

STELLA: You've got the food. Good. (*She takes the parcels from* JOHN WINTER.) I've told you I'm going to cook today's meal?

WINTER: Yes.

STELLA: I want you to take Mr. Southman upstairs to his room now. He is to rest until Mr. Procathren arrives.

WINTER: Very well.

STELLA: Do you hear me, Paul?

PAUL: Yes, but I'm all right.

STELLA: Nevertheless, you're going to rest now.

PAUL: See anything of Procathren in the village, John Winter?

WINTER: No, sir. There's been——

He is interrupted by STELLA. *The following conversations between* JOHN WINTER–STELLA *and* PAUL–CHARLES *take place simultaneously.*

S: This is the meat?

W: Yes.

S: What is it?

W: Beef.

S: We have vegetables.

W: Yes.

S: Will you prepare them?

W: Yes. That's the dried fruit.

S: Good. Where's the coffee?

W: I couldn't get any. That's what I——

S: Why not? We've none at all.

W: I know that. If you'll allow me——

S: I suppose they wouldn't let you have it.

W: There's been trouble in the village.

S: What?

W: There's been trouble in the village.

S: Paul! Charles! Do you hear that?

C: Probably lost his way.

P: No. He's clever.

C: Perhaps he's changed his mind.

P: Why?

C: Decided not to come and see a dirty old man like you.

P: Charles.

C: Yes?

P: I don't want to go to rest.

C: Tell her.

P: You tell her.

C: It'll do you good.

P: You think I ought to go?

C: Yes, I think so.

P: All right.

C: You needn't sleep. You can read.

P: Will you come and read to me?

C: John Winter will. I've found a copy of Alice among my stuff. Would you like that? I'll give it to you for an extra birthday present.

CHARLES: What?

STELLA: Something's happened in the village.

CHARLES: Well, what?

STELLA: Come along, John Winter, let's have it.

WINTER (*He speaks directly to* PAUL.): The reports in the village are confused, sir, but I have been able to gather a little information.

PAUL: Well?

WINTER: Three private soldiers have escaped from a detention camp. They have made their way to the village, and it is believed they slept last night in the village hall. This morning, at an early hour, they broke out of the hall and began marauding and looting the village. Although unarmed they terrorised the villagers. Having obtained food they retired, and are now hiding at some place in the surrounding country.

PAUL: Thank you, John Winter. An excellent and lucid report.

WINTER: Thank you, sir.

STELLA (*to* CHARLES): He'll salute in a moment.

PAUL: Let us appreciate the situation.

STELLA: Surely——

PAUL: Be quiet, Stella. Well, John Winter, have you anything to suggest?

WINTER: I can see no immediate danger to yourself, sir, from the situation at present. By their actions the soldiers have automatically allied themselves with us, although ignorant of our aims and even of our existence. Indeed, by their actions they caused a diversion in the village admirably suited to the day of your visit to London.

PAUL: You think the villagers might have interfered with my going?

WINTER: I had reports to that effect, sir.

PAUL: And you said nothing?

WINTER: I was prepared, sir.

PAUL: The idea of an alliance with these soldiers against the villagers must be considered. Perhaps we could offer this house as——

STELLA: Stop playing at being soldiers yourselves for a minute, and listen to me. You are both going to London today for an express purpose. This is no time to indulge in your fancy for campaigning. (PAUL *and* JOHN WINTER *are silent.*) All right, Captain Winter. Take General Southman to his room.

PAUL: Stella—I——

STELLA: Go along, Grandpa. You can hatch your revolutionary schemes as well up there as you can down here.

> JOHN WINTER *takes* PAUL's *arm and they begin to move to the stairs.*

PAUL: Where's that copy of Alice, Charles?

CHARLES: I'll bring it to you.

STELLA: You're not to read. You're to rest.

PAUL: Charles said I could read.

STELLA: No, you're to rest. (PAUL *and* JOHN WINTER *have gone up the stairs.*) Did you hear them? Ridiculous! Two old men with their stupid attempts at military phrases and reports. Did you hear them? " Situation—immediate danger—diversion—an alliance."

CHARLES: Yes, I heard them.

STELLA: Absurd!

CHARLES: But I thought—I may have been mistaken—I thought that you appreciated a very real danger from the villagers.

STELLA: I do. It is a very real danger. If the villagers could organize themselves, or could be moved by a moment's rage they would come here and kill us all. At present they suffer from no more than a grievance. And they have cause—they have cause for grievance and for hating us. When Paul came here—when he withdrew himself from the world that attacked him—he chose the village to be his butt. I remember the things he said—(*She has taken two loose cigarettes from the pocket of her dress. She throws one to* CHARLES.)—here—catch!—I remember the things he said about the village when I was a child—unforgivable, beastly and unprovoked. Paul was then no longer in a position to attack his equals and so his

E

abuse, the result of hurt pride, was directed against the villagers. It was unprovoked because he had no quarrel with them but for their sanity and security. Soon they felt—under his attack—they felt their security gone and with it their sanity. The satire that had recently shaken the world was directed against them—against a few miserable peasants in a ramshackle hamlet. They reacted in the way of the world, and as Paul would say, " declared war on us ". That war has continued since my childhood. It has coloured my life—the threat of violence to this tortured family. And so, Charles, I am frightened to hear such nonsense talked by Paul—with encouragement from John Winter—when we need expert and serious conspiracy to save our lives. Reason tells us that we cannot fight the villagers—we cannot do it, and so we must get away—run away if you like. That is what we must do. But how? I can do nothing—you can do nothing—we are useless, helpless and wretched and must appeal to the one man capable of saving us—Procathren. I know! I know he is a poor specimen in your eyes, but we must appeal to him. He may help us. You must admit that we need help, and I have no pride in such matters. I have no pride at all. But try to remember, Charles, that I am a woman—try to be conscious of that at other times than when I am naked. I am a woman and I have a child inside me. Does that explain anything to you? Pregnant women have delusions, they say. Do they? I know nothing about it. Am I deluded, Charles? Am I? I only know that I am possessed by a loneliness hard to bear—a loneliness which I should imagine attends forsaken lovers. (*She stands silent—then :*) Lovers. I am innocent of such things. I have imagined what they do and what they say—these lovers. It seems they find a great delight in music and solicitude, in whispering and smiling, in touching and nakedness, in night. And from these things they make a fabric of memory which will serve them well in their life after death when they will be together but alone. They are wise, for that is the purpose

of any memory—of any experience—to give foundation
to the state of death. Understand that whatever we do
today in this house—this damned house—will provide
some of the material for our existence in death and you
understand my fear. No one who has lived as I have
lived could be happy in death. It is impossible. They
speak of us turning in our graves when a slighting word
is spoken of us. No, the words were spoken during our
lifetime, and it is the memory which causes the unrest.
The family—my mother, my father and my sister—out
there in the row of graves—what did they store up, I
wonder? Dadda who fell from grace in the world when
Paul fell and spent the rest of his life living on the charity
of the old man—what does he remember? Mamma—
magnificent angry Mamma—is she happy in the memory
of her justice? Ellen, who died at twenty years, perhaps
happy in the memory of my love for her. As for myself,
if I die today, my eternal happiness will depend on the tiny
memory of you, Charles—you, on your first visit to this
place—standing in the doorway—(*She smiles.*)—consciously picaresque—and handing me the flowers from
your hat. I thought then that we were to be lovers, but
from our marriage you gave me no understanding—no
explanation of the mysteries—only a child conceived in
violence. Therefore, I must ask a stranger. I can use
no female tricks on him. I am not a young girl. I am
unused to laughter and my mind is always slow to understand. I can use neither wit nor beauty. I can only
appeal to his charity to take me away from this place.
Perhaps I can go with him as his servant.

> *She pauses.* CHARLES *is turned away from her. As*
> STELLA *begins to speak again there is a single note
> blown on a trumpet : distant and from the·direction of
> the village.*

Why .don't you speak? Now! Why don't you speak,
now? You could have released me—you could have
freed me from this place if only you could have overcome
your fear of the world out there and returned yourself.

Even now you could kill my black, desperate, damnable fear of all time being empty if you would tell me—show me how to love. I am human and I am a woman. Tell me. And, O, Charles, Charles, comfort me!

He is about to move to her when the trumpet is blown again.
It is nearer and blatant, raucous, defiant. CHARLES *and* STELLA, *hearing this, stare at each other.*

CHARLES: What is it?

STELLA: I don't know.

The trumpet is blown again.

CHARLES: Listen!

PAUL *calls from his room upstairs.*

PAUL: What's that?

STELLA: I don't know, Grandpa. O God! I don't know.

CHARLES: It was nearer.

STELLA: Yes. Nearer.

PAUL: What is it? What is that noise?

The trumpet is being blown.

CURTAIN

ACT TWO

The scene is the same.

The time : four hours later—early afternoon. A fire has been lit.

PAUL *and* STELLA *are sitting at the table ; they have just finished a meal. A place is laid for* CHARLES *who is absent from the room.* JOHN WINTER *is going about clearing away the remains of the meal.*

There is silence until PAUL, *suddenly turning to* STELLA, *asks :*

PAUL: What did you say?

STELLA: Some minutes ago I answered your question and said, "It sounded once more in the distance, then stopped ".

PAUL: What was it?

STELLA: I don't know.

PAUL: It was a trumpet, I know that—but what does it mean? Did you see anything?

STELLA: We didn't look.

> *She puts her face in her hands.*

WINTER: Have you finished with this, sir?

> *He indicates* PAUL'S *plate.*

PAUL: What? Yes. Yes, thank you. (JOHN WINTER *removes the plate.*) Some trick of the villagers, perhaps.

STELLA: They've never dared to come so near to the house before.

PAUL: No. They're getting really mischievous. Did it frighten you?

STELLA: Very much.

PAUL: Mustn't be frightened. (*He stares across the room.*) What's the time?

STELLA: Five and twenty minutes to two.

PAUL: You know, I can't see very well now. It isn't so long ago that I could see that clock from here. Five and twenty minutes to two. (*In silence he takes up a fork and scores deep marks into the tablecloth.*) He's not coming, is he?

STELLA: Procathren?

37

PAUL: Yes.

STELLA: Of course he is. Don't do that. He's probably been——

PAUL: He's changed his mind as Charles said he would. Decided not to come and see me.

STELLA: It's early yet.

PAUL: No. He's changed his mind.

STELLA: Grandpa—would you care very much if he didn't come?

PAUL: Well, yes. Yes, I should be disappointed.

STELLA: Wipe your mouth, darling.

> *He does so.* CHARLES *comes running down the stairs into the room. He carries a book which he throws on to the table before* PAUL.

PAUL: Hullo, Charles!

> *He laughs.*

CHARLES: That's the copy of " Alice in Wonderland " I promised you.

PAUL: Thank you, Charles. Stella, can I have something to drink?

STELLA: Water?

PAUL: Yes, please.

STELLA: Get some water, John Winter.

> JOHN WINTER *goes out to the kitchen with the dishes.* PAUL *sits looking at the book.*

CHARLES: He's not come yet?

> *He stands behind* STELLA *with his hands on her shoulders. Her hands go up to his.*

STELLA: No.

CHARLES: I hope he comes.

STELLA: For my sake?

PAUL: What's that?

CHARLES: Nothing, Paul, nothing.

STELLA: He should have been here by now if they're going to get to London.

CHARLES: Yes. You thought he'd be here for this meal?

STELLA: Yes, I did. I don't know why.

PAUL: Has John Winter brought the water yet?

STELLA: No, not yet. Oh, here it is.

> JOHN WINTER *has entered with a jug of water and some glasses.*

PAUL: I'll pour it out. Have you fed the dog, John Winter?

WINTER: Yes, sir. Some time ago.

PAUL: It must be very cold out of doors. If he wants to come in you are to allow it.

WINTER: He seems to want to stay out.

PAUL: Was he frightened by that noise?

WINTER: I don't know, sir.

CHARLES: Have you heard it again?

STELLA: No. John Winter, will you keep a look-out for Mr. Procathren. I suggest from upstairs.

PAUL: He's not coming!

STELLA: Run along, John Winter.

> JOHN WINTER *goes up the stairs.*

PAUL (*chants*): He's not coming! He's not coming! He's not coming after all, at all.

STELLA: Shut up, Grandpa! And having made so much fuss about the water, why don't you drink it? Charles, I want you to——

> PAUL, *having sipped the water, suddenly reads from the book.*

PAUL: " Once I was a real Turtle." (*He pantomimes a great sigh : the book falls to the floor.*) Then the world wasn't big enough for me to live in. Every time I raised my voice I banged my head. What a fine, brave, gay little chap I was—the world had never seen my like, it said. (CHARLES *and* STELLA *are whispering together.*) How I made them laugh—how they loved me. Have you ever heard —felt the roar of applause—like the thunder of blood in your head? But—pity!——

> Little Southman's come a cropper
> Because he wrote an awful whopper
> Telling Kings and Princes too
> Just how much they ought to do.
> Poor old Paul!
> What a fall!
> Whoo-ah!

That's what they sang when " The Abolition of Printing " had been written and I was on my way here. And
it was true. What a fall! Whoo-ah!

STELLA: Say something, Charles, and stop him rambling.

CHARLES: Boo!

PAUL: What's that? You, who wouldn't say Boo to a goose
dare to say Boo to a Southman? I, who was once a real
Turtle—am I now less than a goose?

STELLA: You're an old goose to talk such nonsense, Paul.

PAUL: Quack-quack!

CHARLES: Whither do you wander?

PAUL: Upstairs and downstairs and in my lady's chamber.

CHARLES: Not any longer, you don't.

PAUL: It's my legs—they've gone weak.

CHARLES: Only your legs?

PAUL: I know what you mean, you dirty boy. Blank cart-
ridge. But you'd have been proud of me once, ducky.
I was full of the stuff of life when I wrote the " Abolition ". Then I went neither upstairs nor downstairs
but straight into my Lady Society's chamber and lifted
the skirts of the old whore. A rough customer—but
she kindly displayed her deformities. Then it was
whoops with the what-d'you-call-'em—Hullo, Mr. So-
and-so!—why, bless me, here's the thingamegig—ssh!—
the tiger's gone into the forest—be a man—be a man—
deliver the goods. (*He snaps his fingers.* ROBERT PRO-
CATHREN *has come up the stairs and is standing in the doorway
of the room. He is unseen by* PAUL, STELLA *amd* CHARLES.)
And when I had performed the obscene gesture what a
rush there was to restore the disarray of the filthy old
bag. What a-neighing and a-braying to assure her that
nothing had been revealed to her detriment. Andrew
Vince pulled up the knickers and John Ussleigh pulled
down the skirts and Arthur Howell took me, the raper,
into custody. The accusation against Paul Frederick
Southman! (*He beats on the arm of his chair.*) " Paul
Frederick Southman: you are charged with the assault
of the well-known and much-beloved whore, Society, in

that you did, with malice and humour, reveal her for what she is and not for what men wish her to be, thereby destroying the illusion of youth and the wisdom of age. Also that you employed the perversion of using for this purpose your pen instead of the recognized organ." Witnesses called for the prosecution. Andrew Vince: this witness testified the poor old body to be sadly shaken by her experience and vehemently denied the defence's suggestion that he had rummaged her after finding her crying in an alley. John Ussleigh: this witness, a publisher, stated that he saw the assault but had been under the impression that it was a case of true love. He had known the prisoner for a number of years, etc., etc. An unnamed young man: this witness, called for medical evidence, admitted intercourse with Society on several occasions. When asked by the defence whether he was not repelled by the malformations of Society, he answered, " I thought all women were like that ". Witnesses called for the defence: none. Sentence: exile.

> *He sees* ROBERT PROCATHREN. *The two men stare at each other across the room.* STELLA *turns to recognize* ROBERT *at once.*

STELLA: Mr. Procathren.

ROBERT: That's right.

STELLA: I'm Stella Heberden.

ROBERT: How do you do.

STELLA: How do you do. This is my grandfather, Paul Southman, and my husband, Charles.

ROBERT: How do you do.

STELLA: Won't you come in?

ROBERT: Thank you. I've left my car some distance away. I could find no road to the house.

STELLA: There isn't one.

ROBERT: I suppose the car will be all right.

STELLA: I'm sure it will be.

> *There is a pause and then* ROBERT *moves towards* PAUL, *and, smiling at him, says :*

ROBERT: Well, sir, this is a great occasion for me.

PAUL: How do you do. Stella!

ROBERT: May I say, Many happy returns of the day.

PAUL: Thank you very much.

ROBERT: I feel there is no necessity for——

CHARLES: Have you had lunch, Mr. Procathren?

ROBERT: What? Yes. Yes, thank you—I have. Surely Mr. Southman, there is no necessity for formality between us on this occasion, but there are a few things I should like to say. Have I your permission?

PAUL is silent.

STELLA: Please go on.

ROBERT: Thank you. I'll be brief. (*He speaks to* PAUL.) What am I doing in coming here today——

PAUL: Did John Winter say he'd fed the dog?

STELLA: Yes, Grandpa. (*To* ROBERT.) You must forgive him.

ROBERT: Of course. I appreciate the honour you do me in allowing me to come here, to this house, today—this house which has been closed to the world for so many years. You withdrew yourself from us, and with yourself your advice and guidance, to punish us for our treatment of you and your ideas. At the time of the attacks on you I was nine years of age and therefore rather too young, actively, to participate in your defence. I have had to wait until today, when I hope—in the following few hours to wipe out the memory of the hatred and violence that was inflicted on you twenty-five years ago by your fellow artists. As a young man my own work was deeply influenced by——

PAUL: What does he say?

ROBERT: No more. I shall say no more. There remains only this: as a material token of our appreciation of your nobility of attitude I have been asked to bring you this book. (*He has taken a leather-bound folio from the brief-case he carries. This book he lays on the table before* PAUL *who makes no attempt to open it.*) With it may I wish you the best of health and happiness and, again, many happy returns of the day.

PAUL nods his head.

STELLA: Well, have a look at the book, Grandpa. (PAUL *shakes his head.*) What do you say? Oh, he hasn't got his glasses.

ROBERT: I'm so sorry. I didn't realize that. May I. (*He takes back the book and opens it.*) In this book you will find some sixty-odd appreciations both in prose and verse— they are all, of course, in autograph. Here are Harold Prospect, Richard Lewis Cameron, Helen Newsome, George Reeves and many others writing in honour of Paul Frederick Southman.

He holds out the book to PAUL.

PAUL: I was a real Turtle once, wasn't I?

He takes the book.

STELLA: Don't be silly, Grandpa.

ROBERT: Now, Mrs. Heberden——

STELLA: Yes?

ROBERT: I don't want to bother Mr. Southman—so may I tell you about the arrangements I have made for today?

STELLA: Certainly.

ROBERT: Well, Mr. Southman will have to walk to the car, I'm afraid—that is possible, isn't it?

STELLA: He has a little cart we sometimes pull him around in—he could use that.

ROBERT: Excellent. Now, we should start from here about four-thirty. (*He looks at the clock—then at his watch.*) Surely your clock is exactly an hour fast.

STELLA: Yes. Yes, it is. It's broken.

ROBERT: We should get to London by seven o'clock giving Mr. Southman time for a short rest before the dinner.

PAUL *and* CHARLES *have been whispering over the book of appreciation. Suddenly* PAUL'S *voice is raised.*

PAUL: No, no, Charles! A very nice young man.

ROBERT *smiles at* STELLA *and continues.*

ROBERT: The dinner will be a formal affair. Many people wish to meet Mr. Southman—I hope it won't tire him— he must say immediately if it does. There will be some speeches—we are hoping that he is going to speak——

STELLA: I think he will—but he's very frightened, you know. (*Very distantly the trumpet sounds.*) It is a fear that he is no longer——

ROBERT: What was that?

STELLA: I heard nothing.

PAUL: There it is again, Stella.

ROBERT: What is it, sir? A barracks?

CHARLES: No. We've no ideas about it, have we, Paul?

> PAUL *and* CHARLES *grin at each other.*

ROBERT: A train, perhaps.

CHARLES: There are no trains round here.

> *There is a pause. Then* ROBERT *laughs, and continues to speak to* STELLA.

ROBERT: I should tell you, Mrs. Heberden, that there will be the presentation of a cheque to Mr. Southman tonight. A certain sum of money has been collected by—What did you say?

STELLA: I said I'd like to speak to you about that.

ROBERT: Certainly.

STELLA: Later. You're leaving at half-past four, Grandpa. (*To* ROBERT.) His man, John Winter, will travel with him. That's all right, isn't it?

ROBERT: Quite all right.

STELLA: So you'll be ready, won't you, Grandpa?

PAUL: Stella!

STELLA: Yes? (*She moves to him.*) It's all right, darling! It's all right. (*She puts her arms around him.*) You see, Mr. Procathren did come after all. (*To* ROBERT.) He was so frightened—so afraid that you weren't coming. Weren't you, darling?

> *She kisses* PAUL.

ROBERT (*going to the mural painting*): This is your work, Mr. Heberden?

CHARLES: Yes.

ROBERT: Interesting. I can't recall seeing anything of yours since the famous show—when was it?—four years ago.

CHARLES: Five.

ROBERT: Five, was it? Anyway, when you were the infant

prodigy startling the country with your engravings to the " Purgatorio ".

CHARLES: That exhibition was a mistake.

ROBERT: For one so young? Perhaps.

CHARLES: I meant otherwise.

ROBERT: If you have any other new work I should be most interested to see it.

CHARLES: For recognition in your literary reviews?

ROBERT: I assure you——

CHARLES: I have nothing. I have ceased to comment upon a society I have forsaken.

ROBERT: But surely, Mr. Heberden, the essence——

CHARLES: Did you have a good journey from London, Mr. Procathren?

ROBERT: I didn't come from London. I came from Oxford.

CHARLES: I see.

ROBERT: I live there.

STELLA: Did you come through the village?

ROBERT: Yes.

STELLA: It was quiet?

ROBERT: There seemed to be no one about—but I drove through very quickly. Why?

STELLA: No reason.

ROBERT: As a matter of fact, I had intended to start earlier and stop in the village to call on the rector. The Reverend Giles Aldus. Do you know him? (*They are silent.*) He has a library—it has been left in his care—a small collection, but it sounds most interesting. You've heard of it, no doubt.

STELLA: No.

ROBERT: No? I was going to call and ask him if I might see it. They are books of a religious nature—almost legendary as they've never been catalogued. Aldus has never allowed it. I'm told he lives with his mother, and both she and the books he keeps from contact with the world. I'm not particularly interested in his mother, but I'd have liked to have seen the books. However, there was time to see neither. By the way, Mrs. Heberden, I must apologize for walking into the house as I did, but I could find no bell or knocker.

CHARLES: We have very few callers.

ROBERT (*He laughs*): I nearly fell over a dog in the doorway. I meant to mention this before. There's a——

STELLA: Oh dear! I hope he didn't annoy you.

ROBERT: No, he didn't annoy me.

PAUL: He doesn't annoy people.

ROBERT: How could he? He's dead. (*There is a pause.* ROBERT *laughs.*) Is that your dog? I didn't know. I thought——

> PAUL *has risen to his feet. He shouts.*

PAUL: John Winter!

STELLA: Paul—Paul!

PAUL (*to* CHARLES): Get John Winter! (CHARLES *is about to move to the stairs when* JOHN WINTER *comes down into the room.*) John Winter!

WINTER: Yes?

PAUL: John Winter, this man says my dog is dead.

WINTER: Where——?

PAUL: This man says my dog is dead.

WINTER: Where is it?

ROBERT: In the doorway—down—— (*He points.*)

> JOHN WINTER *runs from the room.*

PAUL: Help me—Charles, you fool—help me!

STELLA: Paul, you're not to——

> CHARLES *has taken* PAUL'S *arm and is assisting him across the room.*

PAUL: I must go down—I must go down! (*He shouts down the stairs.*) John Winter! Is it true? John Winter, is it true?

> PAUL *and* CHARLES *go from the room to descend the stairs.*

STELLA: O God! O dear Christ!

> *She has moved to the table and, unseeing, beats down with her fist on the presentation book.*

ROBERT: Be careful of that book, please!

STELLA: What?

ROBERT: The book. Please be careful. (*He removes the book*

from under her hand.) I am most distressed, Mrs. Heberden. I had no idea that the dog—you see, I tripped over the carcase and—I thought—well, I really don't know what I thought—the thing was still warm. I must apologize but at the time——

STELLA: —you had something very much more important to think about?

ROBERT: Well, yes.

STELLA: The presentation to Mr. Southman.

ROBERT: Exactly.

STELLA: And I agree, Mr. Procathren.

ROBERT: What? That——

STELLA: That the presentation was more important than a dead dog.

ROBERT: Thank you.

During this conversation between ROBERT *and* STELLA *there is heard from the foot of the stairs at the main door :*

CHARLES (*his voice rising to audibility*): —and we need proof. We don't know anything.

PAUL: Proof! I want no more proof of their intentions. Look at it—look at it—it lies there—dead! Dead!

CHARLES: Paul—Paul! Stop it! (*There is the sound of some heavy object being thrown to the ground.*) Paul—come here! Stop him, John Winter!

The main door of the house is thrown open and PAUL *can be heard shouting.*

PAUL: Come out! Come out, you toads! Why do you hide? You were not afraid of an old dog—why be afraid of an old man? Come out and let me see you!

His last words become a long howl of grief.

STELLA: We must hope—we must pray that——

ROBERT: Yes, Mrs. Heberden?

There is a pause.

STELLA: —that he will go with you this afternoon. I promise he shall go with you. This will make no difference at all. He shall go with you to London, and he will be all right. He will be all right.

ROBERT: We must hope so. Please don't be upset, Mrs. Heberden. I can understand this. An old man—an animal beloved of him——

STELLA: But we must get him away from here soon. You said half-past four——

ROBERT: Yes.

STELLA: It must be before that. As soon as possible. At once!

ROBERT: Very well.

STELLA: He'll arrive early in London, but there must be somewhere he can go, surely.

ROBERT: My flat.

STELLA: He can wait there?

ROBERT: With pleasure.

STELLA: Good.

ROBERT: He'll be all right there, I can assure you. He can rest and during that time——

STELLA: Mr. Procathren.

ROBERT: Yes.

STELLA: Help me.

ROBERT: How?

STELLA: Help me.

ROBERT: In what way?

STELLA: Please!

ROBERT: In what way can I help you?

STELLA: I had prepared what I was going to say to you.

ROBERT: Then please say it.

STELLA: You will help me?

ROBERT: In any way I can, but——

STELLA: There's very little time.

ROBERT: Before they return? I promise to look after the old gentleman, if that's what you mean.

STELLA: Yes. Yes, of course, you must look after him.

ROBERT: I will.

STELLA: Sir! Sir, our future is in your hands.

ROBERT: You must forgive me, I——

STELLA: Our future is in your most beautiful delicate hands.

ROBERT: You must forgive me but I don't understand you.

STELLA: You are young, you are famous and powerful, you are talented and you can do as I ask.

ROBERT (*he laughs*): I am a minor poet—nothing more.

STELLA: Why do you laugh?

ROBERT: I don't know.

STELLA: At this moment—why do you laugh?

ROBERT: Shyness, I suppose. I am shy.

STELLA: I'm sorry but there's no time for the courtesies and formalities as between strangers. You musn't expect them from me. But please don't withdraw. A moment ago you were willing to help me.

ROBERT: I don't understand what you want.

STELLA: This! This is what I want! I want Paul to be restored to his former greatness. In that way there can be a future for my child.

ROBERT: Your child?

STELLA: I'm pregnant. The child Paul. Innocent, you will admit—in no way responsible. For this child's sake old Paul must be restored to greatness in the world.

ROBERT: But he is a great man now. No restoration is necessary.

STELLA: No, he is not a great man now, but——

ROBERT: I came here today to see a great man.

STELLA: —we can restore him. And this is the way. Listen —this is the way.

ROBERT: There is nothing I can do.

STELLA: Nothing can be done today, certainly. Nothing, beyond our having you take him to London. But in the future we can act. You promised to help me——

ROBERT: Really, I——

STELLA: You promised to help me! And you can help me in this way: until you can get us away from this place keep in touch with me—by letter, in person—I'll get away to London to see you if you wish—but by some means— by any means—we must retain contact.

ROBERT: I can see no point in this.

STELLA: Such a small thing to ask. Be gracious, sir—you

F

have so much—be gracious to the poor. (*There is a pause.* ROBERT *turns away.*) What can I offer you?

ROBERT: Nothing.

STELLA: You can be godfather to my child.

ROBERT: I am an atheist.

> *Footsteps can be heard coming up the stairs.*

STELLA: Together we can do so much for Paul. Apart we——

ROBERT (*He has heard the footsteps*): All right!

STELLA: You will help me?

ROBERT: Yes.

STELLA: God bless you!

ROBERT: I'll keep in touch with you by letter but you must instruct me. I've no idea what you intend. They're coming back.

STELLA: I will instruct you, as you put it, in our first letters. It is decided then—you and I can go together now. But I must have a token from you.

ROBERT: A token?

STELLA: A material token. That will do.

> *She indicates the signet ring* ROBERT *is wearing.*

ROBERT: This?

STELLA: Yes. (*She holds out her hand to him. He removes the ring and puts it on a finger of her left hand. As he is doing this* PAUL *comes in the room from below. He moves quickly and breathlessly across the room to the farther stairs.* STELLA *calls to him.*) Paul! (*He does not answer but continues up the stairs to the upper floor.* STELLA *speaks again to* ROBERT.) You mentioned a cheque to be presented.

ROBERT: Yes.

STELLA: It must come to me.

ROBERT: I don't think I can do that.

STELLA: You can contrive some trick.

> ROBERT *still holds* STELLA's *left hand from the giving of the ring.*

ROBERT: Some trick. Is that what you're up to, Mrs. Heberden?

> CHARLES *enters from below.*

CHARLES: Where is he?

STELLA: He's gone to his room. Is the dog dead?

CHARLES: Yes.

STELLA: How is he going to take it?

CHARLES: In anger. Listen! (*There is silence.*) I thought I heard him. (*He smiles at* ROBERT *and* STELLA.) Have you two settled the future?

STELLA: Yes, we have. (*To* ROBERT.) Haven't we?

> ROBERT, *in an agony of embarrassment, moves away from her.*

CHARLES: Excellent! *He laughs.*

STELLA: I'm going to call Paul.

CHARLES: No, Stella—no, let him come down in his own time.

STELLA: You said he was angry. Did you say that?

CHARLES: I did.

STELLA: But why? Why anger?

CHARLES: He's convinced that the villagers poisoned the dog.

STELLA: Did they?

CHARLES: No, I don't think so. It must have died of old age.

STELLA: What a day to choose to die! (CHARLES *is laughing at her.*) It should have waited until tomorrow. (*Suddenly she laughs too, and, continuing to laugh, she speaks.*) It should have waited until tomorrow, when Paul would have been away. However, we must deal with this—this catastrophe. (*She goes to* CHARLES *and puts her hands on his shoulders.*) It will take more than the death of a dog to deter me. You see, Charles, I'm no longer alone. I now have an ally who is prepared with me. Mr. Procathren has promised to help me.

ROBERT: One moment, Mrs. Heberden. I feel I must define the limits of my obligations. They are these: to come here today not only on my own behalf but also on behalf of my committee: to present Mr. Southman with the book of appreciations and our congratulations on his birthday: to drive him to London for the dinner tonight and during that time to accept personal responsibility for his safety: to return him to this house tomorrow. Those are the

limits of my formal obligations—but—I have promised
one thing further—to keep in touch with you by letter
in future. I will do that—but it does not mean, Mrs.
Heberden—(*his voice becomes uncontrolled*)—it does not
mean that I am prepared to become engaged in a partisan
way in any family feud or intrigue. What you are
attempting to do, and how you are attempting to entangle
me—indeed, why—I do not understand. But kindly
remember I have stated my obligations and I am not going
beyond them.

> PAUL *is coming down the stairs into the room.*

CHARLES (*to* STELLA): As an ally I prefer a dead dog.

> PAUL *comes into the room. Beneath his arm he carries a
> large automatic pistol ; he has removed the clip and is
> loading it with cartridges. There is a change in his
> manner. Towards* ROBERT *he is friendly, almost
> familiar, and no longer afraid. He speaks with a clear
> and forceful articulation.*

PAUL: I must admit that even with my daily care of this
weapon I have always looked upon it as being for defence,
never for revenge.

STELLA: What are you going to do?

PAUL: You must forgive me, Mr. Procathren—Robert—
I may call you Robert, may I not?——

ROBERT: Certainly.

PAUL: You must forgive us, Robert, for engaging you in this
business. (*He inserts the magazine into the pistol.*) I trust
your sympathies are with us.

ROBERT: I know nothing of the circumstances, sir.

STELLA: What are you going to do, Grandpa?

PAUL: Whatever I do it will be with this! (*He lays the pistol
down heavily on the table.*) The circumstances, Robert, are
these. For many years past now the occupants of this
house have suffered victimisation by the villagers. The
reason has never been clear to me. Perhaps it is based on
some delusion with regard to our social standing. Perhaps
our being artists—I don't know. But I no longer require
reasons. The act—the act of poisoning my dog—is enough.

STELLA: The dog died of old age.

PAUL: Don't be silly, child. This, Robert, is the first direct move they have made. For years the threat has existed—but, although very real, it was no more than a threat. It lasted so long without action that it became a family joke—eh, Charles?—Stella?—but this is an act and must be answered by as direct and cruel an act. Where is John Winter?

STELLA: I want to know what you are intending to do. Are you forgetting that you go to London today?

PAUL: No, I am not forgetting that—and I shall go.

STELLA: You will?

PAUL: Most certainly. Where is John Winter?

STELLA: He hasn't come up yet. And are you going to London?

PAUL: Don't worry, darling—I shall go. At about four o'clock you said, Robert?

ROBERT: Yes, sir. We should start by then.

PAUL: In that case, I must hurry. Now then—we are one—two—three—four men with John Winter and one woman. With the three soldiers we shall be seven men.

STELLA: Soldiers?

PAUL: The soldiers that have escaped from prison. John Winter mentioned them. The soldiers that have anticipated us in their attack on the village. I propose to form an alliance with them. But, first of all, we must find them. I want you, Charles, to do that—and perhaps you, Robert, would care——

ROBERT: I don't wish to be involved in this, sir.

> There is silence. PAUL stares at ROBERT, his hand going out to touch the pistol. He withdraws and turns to CHARLES.

PAUL: Then you will go with John Winter, Charles. Bring these soldiers back here. I want to talk to them.

ROBERT: Mr. Southman! (PAUL turns to ROBERT.) You must understand my position. I cannot—dare not become engaged in something that is of no personal—no personal——

PAUL: Advantage, Mr. Procathren?

ROBERT: No, sir! Not advantage, but——

PAUL: I have explained the circumstances to you. You are an intelligent man—you have undoubtedly understood. Will you or will you not help me?

ROBERT: My personal position——

PAUL: I don't understand your doubt and hesitation. With your admiration of myself surely you believe what I have told you to be true.

ROBERT: Of course.

PAUL: We need your help.

ROBERT: I will help you in any indirect way that I can——

PAUL: No qualifications! Will you or will you not help me? I shall not ask again. *There is a pause.*

ROBERT: I will.

STELLA: You are being untrue to me!

ROBERT: What can I do? What else can I do?

STELLA (*she cries out*): Then what is going to happen? (*There is a complete cessation of activity whilst* STELLA *speaks. She is swept by a sudden storm of fore-knowledge, awful in its clarity. The men, silent and unmoving, watch her.*) Careful! We are approaching the point of deviation. At one moment there is laughter and conversation and a progression: people move and speak smoothly and casually, their breathing is controlled and they know what they do. Then there occurs a call from another room, the realization that a member of the assembly is missing, the sudden shout into the dream and the waking to find the body with the failing heart lying in the corridor—with the twisted limbs at the foot of the stairs—the man hanging from the beam, or the child floating drowned in the garden pool. Careful! Be careful! We are approaching that point. The moment of the call from another room. (*She pauses.*) Give me another of your cigarettes, Paul.

PAUL: What was it, my darling?

STELLA: Give me a cigarette.

> PAUL *takes the box from his pocket and hands it to* STELLA.

PAUL: We are aware, my dear—stop it! you're trembling—
yes, we are aware——

STELLA: Damn!

> *She throws away the match with which she is attempting to
> light her cigarette.* ROBERT *steps forward and lights
> it for her as* PAUL *continues to speak.*

PAUL: —very much aware of the menace of the point of
deviation. We are eagerly awaiting the shout from
another room for we know from whom it will come and
to whom it will be directed. Also we are aware of the
discovery—the destruction of the village—and so we have
nothing to fear. All we have to do is to wait a little
while—(JOHN WINTER *comes into the room from below.*)—
but apparently, not long. Yes, John Winter?

WINTER: There's a gentleman to see you, sir.

PAUL: The whole world is calling on us today. Who is it?

WINTER: From the village.

PAUL: Ah, well?

WINTER: The Reverend Aldus.

PAUL: The holy book-worm, eh? Tell him to come up.
(JOHN WINTER *turns and shouts down the stairs,* "*Will you
come up, please* ".) What does this mean? If they think
I can't attack clerics they should remember my history.
Now for it.

> *The* REVEREND ALDUS *comes into the room.* JOHN
> WINTER *goes out.*

ALDUS: Good afternoon. (PAUL *inclines his head but is silent.
The others whisper,* "*Good afternoon* ".) My name is Aldus.

PAUL: I am Southman. This is my grand-daughter, Stella,
her husband, Charles Heberden, and a friend and sympa-
thizer, Mr. Robert Procathren. (ALDUS *nods to each in
turn.*) Please sit down.

ALDUS: Thank you.

PAUL: You will notice, my dears, first of all, the general
attitude. That of humility bordering on servility. It
is dangerous to the unwary. It has been used by the
Church for hundreds of years to gain advantage in a
situation such as this. Next, notice the facial expression.

A cursory examination and one might take it to be shyness, perhaps idiocy. It is neither. The clothes, notice the clothes. And the posture—neat, precise. If you were to go near him you would smell not sanctity but intrigue. But don't go near him. I forbid it.

There is a pause.

ALDUS (*he has a marked impediment in his speech*): May I speak?

PAUL: Certainly.

ALDUS: You have finished your attack?

PAUL: I have not yet begun.

ALDUS: It is evident, Mr. Southman, that I cannot match your fluency in this conversation. I am forced, by my disability, to select only certain words for my use.

PAUL (*he laughs*): You're doing very well. Carry on.

ALDUS: I have a proposal.

PAUL: Concerning the soldiers?

ALDUS: Yes. You've heard——?

PAUL: Partly. Tell us—in well-selected words—what has happened—and what you propose.

ALDUS: Late last night these three men came to see me at the Rectory. I was alone. Their leader—— (*The trumpet sounds from the middle distance.*) Listen!

PAUL: Yes, we've heard it. Is that the soldiers?

ALDUS: Yes.

PAUL: Apparently we were mistaken. We thought it was your people fooling about.

ALDUS: No, it is the soldiers. I will tell you. These men came to me—they were honest in that they explained the true position—their escape from criminal detention—it was I who practised dishonesty—and by that I have brought——

PAUL: Get on, man! There's little time. Certainly no time for self-examination.

ALDUS: Forgive me. Their leader asked one thing of me—shelter for the night. I agreed, and told them that they could sleep in the church hall. They went there. They trusted me. In the early hours of the morning I got up

and—moved by some sense of justice outside my province
—I—— *He is in tears.*

PAUL: Come along. What is it?

ALDUS: I say, forgive me. My mother——

PAUL: Never mind your mother now. Tell us about the soldiers.

ALDUS: I got up and went to the hall and locked them in. I locked the soldiers in.

> *Very sharply and suddenly, but shortly* PAUL *and* CHARLES *laugh.*

PAUL: What happened then?

ALDUS: They broke out of the hall just before daylight. One of them had stolen a trumpet from among some band instruments that were stored there. That is the trumpet you can hear. With that they are advertising their presence. (*He has risen from his chair.*) They are marauding through the countryside. The village is terrorised. They attacked the baker——

PAUL: Why the baker?

ALDUS: There seems to be no reason for their acts. They are madmen. I do not understand! I do not understand!
> *He is shouting and stammering incoherently.*

PAUL: Be quiet! (*Then, in silence*) What do you expect of me?

ALDUS: Come to—come to ask your help, sir.

PAUL: You've what?

ALDUS: Come to ask your help, sir.

PAUL: Against the soldiers?

ALDUS: Yes, sir.

PAUL: I see. How long have you lived in the village, Mr. Aldus?

ALDUS: Five years.

PAUL: Five years. Please sit down. Then you know the situation that exists—has always existed between the village and this house?

ALDUS: Yes, sir.

PAUL: You do?

ALDUS: Yes.

PAUL: And yet you come to ask my help?

ALDUS: I know the history of hatred, sir, and yet I appeal to you in my weakness to help us against these men.

PAUL: You turn in your weakness to me, Mr. Aldus? You surprise me.

ALDUS: Mr. Southman!

PAUL: Telephone for the police.

ALDUS: They destroyed the telephone lines last night.

PAUL: Send one of your young men as a runner.

ALDUS: You know we have no young men among us.

PAUL: And I have two.

ALDUS: Yes.

PAUL: And one of them has a car. Have you tried prayer?

ALDUS: Sir! Sir, we cannot——

PAUL: Have you tried appeasement? Offer them——

ALDUS: We cannot——

PAUL: Have you tried preaching? Appeal to their better natures! (ALDUS *has foundered upon his incoherence. He is silent*.) And so you have come to me. Why?

ALDUS: Because, by reputation, you are a great and powerful man.

PAUL: Thank you.

ALDUS: A man——

PAUL: Would you say a good man, Mr. Aldus? (ALDUS *is silent*.) Ah! then you would use evil to combat evil. A strange presumption for one of your ridiculous uniform.

ALDUS: I cannot engage in polemics with you.

PAUL: Very well. You ask me to lead you against these men to achieve—what?

ALDUS: To uphold law and order; to protect the people of my village.

PAUL: Are you not thinking more of your books? Of the danger to your precious books.

ALDUS: No.

PAUL: Are you sure? I heard what Robert said—he didn't think I was listening, but I heard of all your books about God. Think, Mr. Aldus! Perhaps you now love the books more than you love God.

ALDUS: No.

PAUL: That would be very wrong, Mr. Aldus. Very wrong indeed.

ALDUS: I am thinking of the villagers—of the people. I am thinking——

PAUL: You are? I just thought it might not be so. It is for them you want help?

ALDUS: Yes.

PAUL: Ask me.

ALDUS: What?

PAUL: To help you.

ALDUS: Help us.

PAUL: Properly.

ALDUS: Will you help us?

PAUL: No.

ALDUS: There could only——

PAUL: Again!

ALDUS: What?

PAUL: Ask again.

STELLA: Paul!

PAUL: Shut up! Ask again.

ALDUS: Will you help us?

PAUL: No! (*He has taken up the pistol. He goes to* ALDUS *and taps him on the chest with the barrel of the weapon.*) No! I will not help you. I shall form an alliance however—oh, yes, I shall do that—but it will be with the soldiers and with them I shall revenge myself upon you and your impudent mob. (*He turns away.*) Go! Leave us! Will someone show Mr. Aldus to the door.

STELLA *moves to* ALDUS.

CHARLES: I'll go with him.

STELLA: No, I'll go. (*She takes* ALDUS *by the arm.*) Will you be able to get back all right?

ALDUS *nods. They reach the door when* ALDUS *turns.*

ALDUS: Mr. Southman, I will dare to say to you——

But PAUL *who has been performing a little silent dance, interrupts* ALDUS *by pointing the pistol at him, squinting along the barrel, and saying:*

PAUL: Bang! (ALDUS *and* STELLA *go out.* PAUL *moves to a position between* ROBERT *and* CHARLES. *He puts his arms about them.*) Well, my dear Robert—and my very dear Charles, that pathetic creature has been sent us to represent our enemy. Not very flattering, is it?

CHARLES (*he is laughing*): What are you going to do?

PAUL: Charles, no! We must be serious. (CHARLES *is silent.*) We musn't allow what we've just seen—an awful display of fear, non-comprehension and self-conscious pathos—we musn't allow that to make us laugh or to make us pity. It is an old trick, and we are human. He wanted to tell us about his mother. She is dead—or dying—or doesn't love him any longer—is angry with him, perhaps, for his part in this business—but I wouldn't allow him to speak of it. It might be that there is really some tragedy, and we cannot allow ourselves to be diverted by sympathy for such things. No, Charles—even though they had sent us the whole circus instead of the solitary clown we must not be amused or allow our emotions to be touched in any way. (*He pauses.*) What am I going to do, you ask? What am I going to do? (*The action becomes centred on* ROBERT PROCATHREN—PAUL *and* CHARLES *towards* ROBERT. *The three men move and speak at extreme speed.* PAUL *savagely and in great exaltation :* CHARLES *amusedly and lightly, foreseeing towards what they are moving although not the actual event :* ROBERT *through fear, attempting to join in the fantastic jollity as he attempted to join in games and horseplay when a schoolboy.*) Can you fight, Robert?

ROBERT: Well, sir, I——

PAUL: If you can't——

CHARLES: —we haven't much time to teach you.

PAUL: No.

ROBERT: A little boxing when I was at school.

> PAUL *and* CHARLES *laugh with delight.*

CHARLES: Always the little boys, was it?

PAUL: The boys a little smaller than you——

CHARLES: —but not too obviously smaller.

PAUL: Poor little bastards! I bet you punished them. No, I meant——

CHARLES: I've been told there are rules to that sort of thing.

> *He has jumped upon the table and taken up an attitude of defence.*

PAUL: Shut up, Charles! No, Robert, I meant——

CHARLES: You musn't kick, must you?

PAUL: I meant, Robert, fighting. With weapons. Such as this. *He holds up the pistol.*

ROBERT: No. I've had no experience of such things.

PAUL: Never?

ROBERT: Never.

CHARLES: But surely——

PAUL: Could you learn?

CHARLES: Surely you must have been engaged in some war—

ROBERT: No.

CHARLES: —at your age.

ROBERT: No. I was not fit.

CHARLES: Morally or physically?

ROBERT: Both.

CHARLES: You fought with your pen, eh?

PAUL: Have you never——

CHARLES: Poems of victory!

ROBERT: And defeat.

PAUL: Have you never been moved——

CHARLES: Bravo!

PAUL: —moved by hate or persecution——

CHARLES: Or love?

PAUL: —to contemplate physical violence?

ROBERT: Never.

CHARLES: It has always been unemotional, calm force——

PAUL: —in boxing rings——

CHARLES: —with rules——

PAUL: —and referees——

CHARLES: —against harmless little boys.

PAUL: Do you think you could use this?

> *He holds out the pistol to* ROBERT.

ROBERT: I've never handled one before.

> *He takes the pistol from* PAUL.

PAUL: Will you use it——

CHARLES: It is simple!

PAUL: —with us against the villagers?

CHARLES: Oh, so very simple!

ROBERT: Yes, I'll use it.

PAUL: Against the villagers?

ROBERT: Yes.

PAUL: It's loaded.

> ROBERT *raises the pistol to point at* PAUL *and* CHARLES.

CHARLES: Look out!

> PAUL *and* CHARLES *raise their hands above their heads in
> mock terror and then shout with laughter.*

ROBERT (*smiling*): Sorry.   *He turns away*

PAUL: There's a catch——

CHARLES: There's a catch in everything, Robert.

PAUL: —at the side of the butt.

CHARLES: Which is the bit you are now holding.

PAUL: You release the catch to fire.

CHARLES: Then slight pressure on the trigger——

PAUL: Face away, dear boy, face away!

CHARLES: That releases the striker which explodes the cap
which ignites the powder which, expanding as gas, forces
out the bullet——

PAUL: Which brings down the house that Paul built!

CHARLES: Isn't that better——

PAUL: Bang! Bang!

CHARLES: —and simpler——

PAUL: Bang!

CHARLES: —then your boxing with bare fists?

ROBERT: You must explain the method by which—— (*The
pistol goes off in his hand.* PAUL *and* CHARLES *shout with
laughter again.* ROBERT, *dropping the pistol to the floor,
stands holding his wrist.*) O God!

PAUL: Oh dear, no, Robert! Not that way at all.

CHARLES: No. You must be conscious of when you
fire——

PAUL: —and of the direction in which you fire. Oh, yes, you must be much more careful. It is simple, but not as simple as that. The agency is human, not providential. But at least you can fire it—accuracy will come.

> CHARLES *has taken up the pistol from the floor. He removes the clip of remaining cartridges and holds out the pistol to* ROBERT.

CHARLES: There you are. Now you can play with it.

ROBERT: I don't want it! I don't want it!

PAUL: It's all right now. Unloaded.

CHARLES: Of course it is.

PAUL: Take hold of it and we'll have a little drill.

ROBERT: I don't want it!

CHARLES: But it's perfectly safe now. Look!

> *He thrusts the pistol into* ROBERT'S *face and pulls the trigger. The striker clicks : nothing more.* ROBERT *after a pause, takes the pistol from* CHARLES.

PAUL: That's right. Now—— (*From almost immediately below the windows, in the garden, there is a great blast blown on the trumpet.*) Listen! They're here—the soldiers! (*He runs to the window.*) Our allies. They're here. They'll know how to use that.   *He is laughing.*

CHARLES: Can you see them?

PAUL: No. Perhaps my eyes—I can see nobody. (*He opens the window.*) But they're here. (*He shouts.*) Don't be afraid. Come out—come up here. You're welcome. You're welcome!

CHARLES: Can you see them?

PAUL: No. There's nobody. Nobody at all.

CHARLES: Shout again.

PAUL: Don't be afraid. We are friends. We are enemies to the village. Come up—come up!

> *The three men listen in silence and into that silence comes the voice of* JOHN WINTER *shouting from the foot of the stairs at the main door.*

WINTER: Mr. Southman—Mr. Southman, sir!

PAUL (*shouting*): We are friends, I assure you. We wish you well. Bless you, I say, bless oh bless you!

Again they listen and again JOHN WINTER *shouts : this time from just beyond the door.*

WINTER: Mr. Southman!

PAUL: What is it? What does John Winter want?

CHARLES: I don't know.

WINTER: Mr. Southman!

ROBERT: Fools! You fools! Don't you understand? Don't you understand—that is the shout from another room.

PAUL: What?

ROBERT: The shout from another room—that is it. That! Have you forgotten?

CHARLES: Where's Stella?

PAUL: The shout from another room?——

CHARLES: Where's Stella?

ROBERT: Yes. Where is Stella?

CHARLES: She went to show Aldus out.

ROBERT: She should be back, shouldn't she?

CHARLES: Yes.

ROBERT: Well, where is she now? Where is she now?

CHARLES: Stella!

> *He runs to the door—for a moment he pauses and then, decided, he begins to open the door. It opens a few inches but that is all : there is some obstruction at the other side.*

PAUL (*shouting to the soldiers*): Gentlemen, I assure you that we are friends. Come up here and let us talk——

CHARLES: Paul—what is wrong? Why won't the door open? John Winter!

> PAUL *leaves the window and comes back into the room.*

PAUL: What is it? What are you doing?

CHARLES: Why won't the door open? The door—what is the matter with the door? Help me!

> *But in the moment's pause when neither* PAUL *nor* ROBERT *move* CHARLES *has thrown the full weight of his body against the door. The door opens fully and* CHARLES, *still within the room, stands looking down at the stairs. He cries out then again, the second time the sound resolving itself into the name,* Stella.

PAUL: What? What? (CHARLES *runs from the room on to the stairs.* PAUL *stands plucking at* ROBERT's *sleeve.*) What is it? What is wrong, Robert? What has gone wrong?

> ROBERT *motionless, does not answer him.* CHARLES *calls from the stairs.*

CHARLES: Help me! Help me!

> PAUL *goes from the room on to the stairs.* ROBERT *left alone, holding the empty pistol, does not move. He does not look towards the door.* PAUL, *looking down at the stairs, backs into the room.* CHARLES *and* JOHN WINTER *come in carrying* STELLA : *she is dead. For a time the group is still and silent—then* JOHN WINTER *speaks.*

WINTER: Put her down, sir. (CHARLES *does not move. He stares down into* STELLA's *face.*) Mr. Heberden. Put her down, sir. We must see——

PAUL: Stella. Stella. Stella.

WINTER: Put her down, sir.

> *They lay the body on the floor.*

PAUL: Robert—Stella's hurt.

WINTER: May I——? Mr. Heberden, may I look at her?

> CHARLES *nods his head. He moves quickly to the door. He finds the bullet-hole.*

PAUL: Or is it a joke? They've played jokes on me before. (JOHN WINTER *opens the bodice of* STELLA's *dress, exposing her breasts.*) You wouldn't play jokes on me, Robert. That would be cruel. You wouldn't ridicule me. No, she's playing the joke on me. Stella—Stella darling, stop it. It's not a very good joke.

WINTER: There is a bullet wound—here.

PAUL: Stella!

WINTER: It has, I think, passed through her heart.

PAUL: What do you say, John Winter?

WINTER: There is no pulse.

PAUL: John Winter! You dare to enter into this joke?

WINTER: She is dead.

CHARLES: Dead.

PAUL: Dead! You go too far, sir. Leave the room!

CHARLES: John Winter says she is dead. Shot dead.

PAUL: Dead. Dead. The doors are shutting in the empty house. Dead. Dead.

WINTER: Who was it? I heard the shot. (CHARLES *without turning his head, points to* ROBERT *who, with the empty pistol half-raised has not moved.*) But why? Why?

PAUL: Won't any of you speak to me? I am at fault, I suppose. Listen—I'll confess. You've frightened me. There—I've admitted it. You've frightened me with your joke. Now speak to me.

WINTER (*to* CHARLES): Shall we take her upstairs, sir?

PAUL: Speak to me.

WINTER (*to* CHARLES): Shall we take her upstairs, sir? Nothing can be done.

PAUL: Nothing can be done. (CHARLES *and* JOHN WINTER *lift* STELLA'S *body from the floor. They begin to carry her to the stairs leading to the upper floor.*) Nothing can be done. (PAUL *follows* CHARLES *and* JOHN WINTER.) Don't go, Robert. I'll be down in a minute when I've settled this and then I'll show you how to use the pistol properly. A fine business, indeed. (CHARLES *and* JOHN WINTER *are going up the stairs.*) Wait for me. Where are you taking my darling? Wait for me.

> CHARLES *and* JOHN WINTER, *carrying* STELLA'S *body between them, have gone up the stairs from the room. From the foot of the iron steps leading from the balcony to the garden comes a piercing human whistle piping a popular tune. It does not disturb* ROBERT *who remains motionless, and* PAUL *has followed* CHARLES *and* JOHN WINTER *from the room. There is the sound of heavy boots on the iron steps. On to the balcony and so into the room by the window come three soldiers—*WALTER KILLEEN, HENRY CHATER *and their leader* CHRISTIAN MELROSE. HENRY CHATER *carries a trumpet. It is* WALTER KILLEEN *who is whistling, but he stops as they enter the room to stand a little inside the window.* ROBERT, *unmoving, has his back to them.*

MELROSE: Good afternoon. I hear we're welcome in this

house. That'll be a change. (ROBERT *does not move.*
MELROSE *raises his voice.*) Good afternoon. (*It is when*
ROBERT *turns that* MELROSE *sees the pistol in his hand.*) A
nice welcome. A very nice welcome, indeed! (*To*
CHATER *and* KILLEEN.) Don't move (*To* ROBERT.) And
what are you going to do with that?

ROBERT: What?

MELROSE: You have a pistol in your hand.

ROBERT: What do you say?

MELROSE: Are you deaf? I said, You have a pistol in your
hand.

ROBERT: Oh, yes. It's not loaded—now.

MELROSE: I'm very happy to hear that. Very happy, indeed.
(*He takes the pistol from* ROBERT, *examines it and puts it on
the table.*) I thought—just for a minute, you know—I
thought we weren't welcome here. (*To* KILLEEN *and*
CHATER.) Come in—sit down—don't fool about. Keep
quiet. You can sit there, and you sit there, where I can
see you. (KILLEEN *and* CHATER *come into the room and sit
down.* MELROSE *turns back to* ROBERT.) Who are you?
What's your name?

ROBERT: Procathren.

MELROSE: What?

ROBERT: Procathren. Robert Procathren.

MELROSE: Robert, is it? I'll call you Bob—or perhaps Bobby
would be better. I'm Melrose—1535380 Christian—my
name not my faith. This is Killeen, and this, Chater.
Stand up! (KILLEEN *and* CHATER *stand up and perform
magnificent mock bows to* ROBERT.) That's better. Once
upon a time, although you wouldn't think it to look at
us, we were soldiers.

ROBERT: Yes, I've heard about you.

MELROSE: Oh, you've heard about us. Then that saves a lot
of explaining, doesn't it? About why we're here and——

ROBERT: Yes. You needn't explain.

MELROSE: Thank you very much. But you can explain something to me. Why are you all dressed up?

ROBERT: I was on an errand.

MELROSE: Do you always put on your best clothes to run errands? What's your job?

ROBERT: I'm a poet.

MELROSE: A poet. (*To* KILLEEN *and* CHATER.) He's a poet.

> MELROSE *is about to speak but* KILLEEN *has risen and recites.*

KILLEEN: Oh it was down by the river
          That I made her quiver
          Oh, you should have seen her belly
          It was shaking like a jelly
          Oh, you should have seen her——

MELROSE: That's enough! (KILLEEN *sits down.*) Give us your professional opinion, Bobby. Isn't that lovely poetry? Well—(*he laughs*)—never mind. Do you live here?

ROBERT: No.

MELROSE: What are you doing here, then? You don't look right. You don't—— (CHATER *blows softly on the trumpet.* MELROSE *turns on him.*) Listen! I've told you about blowing on it when I'm talking. So shut up or I'll take it away from you. Do you hear? I'll take it right away from you—so shut it! (*To* ROBERT.) Who lives here, then?

ROBERT: The Southman family.

MELROSE: I see. Who was it called to us from the window?

ROBERT: Paul—the old man.

MELROSE: What is he?

ROBERT: A poet.

MELROSE: Birds of a feather, eh?

ROBERT: No!

MELROSE: Well, don't shout. (*He has taken out a packet of cigarettes.*) Have one?

ROBERT: No, thank you.

MELROSE: Well, Bobby, I'm afraid we must be getting on.

ROBERT: No, don't go! Don't go!

MELROSE: What?

KILLEEN: Hey, Christy?

> *He has been staring at the painting on the wall.*

MELROSE: Wait a minute. Why don't you want us to go, Bobby? Come on, tell me—I'm interested. People usually want us to move on as quickly as possible. But you want us to stay. Now, why is that?

KILLEEN: Hey, Christy!

MELROSE: Well, what is it?

KILLEEN: Look! *He points to the painting.*

MELROSE: Well, what about it? It's a painting—done with brushes, you know.

KILLEEN: Hey, but Christy—look, look!

MELROSE: I'm looking.

KILLEEN: What is it?

MELROSE and KILLEEN move to stand before the painting.

MELROSE: Well, what's your guess?

KILLEEN: It's as good as yours. Look!

He extends a finger.

MELROSE: Don't touch!

KILLEEN: All right.

MELROSE: Well, don't touch. It isn't finished. Look—(*he rubs his fingers into the paint*)—here. It isn't finished.

KILLEEN: There's some paint—let's finish it.

MELROSE: No! (*They stand looking up at the painting. Then MELROSE, without turning, asks:*) Are there any women here? (*ROBERT, unaware that he cannot be seen, shakes his head.*) I said, Are there any women here?

ROBERT: There was one.

MELROSE: Oh?

ROBERT: I killed her.

MELROSE: What?

ROBERT: I killed her.

MELROSE: Wasn't that rather a silly thing to do?—when there was only one, I mean.

ROBERT: She was horrible—she was pregnant——

MELROSE: I see.

ROBERT: —but it was an accident.

MELROSE: Is that why you asked us not to go?

ROBERT: Yes. (*There is a silence as the THREE SOLDIERS stare at ROBERT. Then ROBERT, stretching out his hands before him, seems to be about to fall.*) What have they made me do?

> MELROSE *goes to him and holds him.*

MELROSE: Hold up! Hold up, you're all right. Killeen, get the cure-all. (KILLEEN *goes to a small haversack he has been carrying and takes out a bottle of whisky.*) Now, come along, Bobby, you're all right.

ROBERT: Oh, what have they made me do?

> MELROSE *takes the whisky from* KILLEEN.

MELROSE: Here—have some of this. Spoils of war.

ROBERT: No.

MELROSE: Oh, don't be an old woman! Go on. (ROBERT *drinks from the bottle.*) Careful! You're dribbling it. Better? Nothing like it, is there? What are you afraid of, Bobby?

ROBERT: Of what is going to happen.

MELROSE: We won't let anything happen to you. Will we? (*He turns to* CHATER *who, with the trumpet across his knees, is peaceably picking his nose.*) Happy?

> CHATER *grins.*

ROBERT: You'll help me?

MELROSE: Of course. (*He holds out the bottle of whisky.*) Have some more. We've got another bottle.

> *He winks at* KILLEEN *and* CHATER.

ROBERT: You will help me?

MELROSE: I've said, yes. Go on, drink up.

ROBERT: Oh, my dear friend, they have made me do dreadful things. But you will help me?

MELROSE: Yes.

ROBERT: Thank God for you!

MELROSE: Yes, indeed.

ROBERT: We must plan what we shall do.

MELROSE: Yes, we will—we will.

ROBERT: Then let us go.

MELROSE: You're going to run away?

ROBERT: No, my friend, I'm going to run towards the event. A thing I have never done before—but now I have the authority. Let us go.

MELROSE: Where to?

ROBERT: First, the village.

MELROSE: All right.

      PAUL *calls from an upper room.* Then nothing can be done! Nothing! And it is no joke—no joke!

ROBERT (*whispers*): No joke.

MELROSE: The old man?

ROBERT: Yes.

MELROSE: With the woman?

ROBERT: Yes.

MELROSE: Should I go up?

ROBERT: No! No!

MELROSE: All right.

ROBERT: You can trust me.

MELROSE: I'm sure I can.

ROBERT: It will all be for the best.

MELROSE: I'm sure it will.

      He looks at KILLEEN *and puts his finger to his forehead. They laugh.*

ROBERT: Let us go.

      MELROSE *picks up the pistol from the table.*

MELROSE: I'll take this.

ROBERT (*to* CHATER): Sound the trumpet! (CHATER, *standing, raises the trumpet smartly and blows a single sustained note.* ROBERT *looks towards the stairs.*) Ready?

MELROSE: Ready.

      MELROSE, CHATER *and* KILLEEN *move to the window, out on to the balcony and so down into the garden.* ROBERT *is about to follow them and has reached the window when* PAUL *comes down the stairs.*

PAUL: Robert!

ROBERT: I am here.

PAUL: It's no joke.

ROBERT: Indeed, it is no joke. No joke at all.

      He is crouched by the window, one arm outstretched to support himself.

PAUL: She's dead.

ROBERT: Yes. Quite, quite dead.

PAUL: You killed her.
ROBERT: I did.
PAUL: Why, Robert?

ROBERT *is staring at* PAUL.

ROBERT: Beast-face!
PAUL: Robert!
ROBERT: Beast-face!
PAUL: Robert!
ROBERT: Satisfied? Satisfied by the shift of responsibility, eh?
PAUL: Robert!
ROBERT: Shan't step from under it this time. Surprised, eh?
PAUL: Robert! (*But* ROBERT *has gone, running down the steps to the garden after the soldiers.* PAUL *moves to the window.*) Robert, come back! I have forgiven you—I have forgiven you! (*But* PAUL *can no longer be seen or heard by* ROBERT. PAUL *turns back into the room.*) I have forgiven him.

> *Then, alone and old, he is seized by a terrible paroxysm of grief and fear. His eyes are closed: from his mouth comes a thin sound: his hands go up and tear the scarf from his neck. It is as if he would do himself great physical violence but his strength fails him—he can only stand exhausted.*

CURTAIN

ACT THREE

The scene is the same.

The time is six hours later : it is night.

CHARLES *is working on the mural painting. He has gathered the lamps of the room around him and light is so concentrated on his work. His model is the body of Stella which lies on an improvised bier on the rostrum before the painting. The body is draped but for the face and head. On the floor, at the foot of the bier, lies a collection of human and animal bones. The painting on the wall is almost complete for* CHARLES *has added the figure of Stella as she lies in death. The other figures now look down at her and the dog stands at her head.*

At the other side of the room about the fireplace and in darkness but for the firelight are five women and a child. HANNAH TREWIN, MARGARET BANT, EDITH TINSON *and* FLORA BALDON *are old. The other woman, who is young, is* JUDITH WARDEN— *mother of the* CHILD *who stands at her side. This* CHILD, *a girl, is ten years of age. She is dressed, fortuitously, as though for some celebration ; although she wears a large pair of boots and a pair of boy's long trousers she also wears a short white embroidered frock of satin. A gay scarf is tied about her head to frame her face and also on her head is a yellow straw hat decorated with tiny artificial flowers. Each of the women in this group carries, wears, or has placed on the floor by her feet some of the surprising objects taken by those flying from a catastrophe. In this case there is a large shining china jug, a gramophone, an oleograph of a scene from " Romeo and Juliet " and various nondescript bundles.* EDITH TINSON *has two pairs of shoes slung round her neck by a length of string.* MARGARET BANT *carries an ornate parasol, and is hung about with an excessive amount of cheap jewellery.* HANNAH TREWIN *appears to be wearing at least three hats. These things, quite worthless to these people in their present predicament, were snatched up in the last desperate moment. The group is silent and motionless but for the* CHILD *who bounces a rubber ball against the door.*

Through the windows the visible expanse of sky is red : the village is burning. It is this fire that JOHN WINTER *stands by the window to watch.*

The tolling of church bells can be heard.

WINTER: It doesn't look as if he'll be able to sound the bells much longer.

CHARLES: Why?

WINTER: I can see the tower now—very black against the fire—very near—not much longer.

CHARLES: The sooner the better—damned noise.

> *The* CHILD *is restrained by her* MOTHER *from bouncing the ball.*

WINTER: What do they hope to gain by ringing the bells?

CHARLES: Help, I suppose.

WINTER: From God?

CHARLES: God alone knows! (*They smile at each other.*) Where's Paul?

WINTER: Upstairs, sir. Packing.

CHARLES: Packing?

WINTER: Packing his bag.

CHARLES: Does he think he's still expected to go?

WINTER: He seems to have no doubt, sir. I'm afraid he's very ill.

CHARLES: Oh, don't put it like that. Say he's going mad, nuts, bats, potty but not that he's very ill.

WINTER: I'm sorry, sir. I tried to explain that he's no longer expected to go to London today and that Procathren may——

CHARLES: What did Procathren say to the old man before he went? That's what I'd like to know.

> PAUL *calls from an upper room :*

PAUL: The village is burning away. There'll be nothing left as far as I can see—nothing at all.

CHARLES: Why isn't there more light?

WINTER: Shall I get you candles?

CHARLES: No! Don't leave the room. I can see. I can see. (JOHN WINTER *begins to make a rearrangement of the lamps.*) There's someone out there!

WINTER: Where?

CHARLES: Out on the balcony.

> JOHN WINTER *turns to stare out of the window.*

WINTER: Yes. (*He raps on the window and then, opening it, calls :*) Come along! Come along in here. It's all right— don't be frightened.

CHARLES: Who is it?

WINTER (*he laughs*): Old Cowper, the postman. Chk-chk-chk-chk-chk! (*he says as if calling an animal.*) Come on. Come on. Come on.

> THOMAS COWPER *appears at the window. He is in the uniform of a country postman and carries his mail delivery bag.*

COWPER: What do you mean, chk-chk-chk-chk-chk, indeed. Do you think I'm afraid to come in here? If so, let me say I'm as good as any that lives in this damned house and what's more, I'm here in the course of my duty and you are at the moment impeding that duty. Get out of the way! (JOHN WINTER *steps aside and* COWPER *marches into the room and goes to* JUDITH WARDEN, *holding out a letter to her.*) For you, Mrs. Warden, my dear. I've been looking for you all evening—your house has quite gone so I couldn't leave it there. But they told me you'd come this way It's from your husband, my dear. Well, that's the last one. (*He takes off his cap and turns to* CHARLES.) Now then, young man. Stop that—whatever it is you're doing. I want a few details from you.

CHARLES: Details?

COWPER: Yes.

> *He has taken a notebook from his pocket and has a pencil ready.*

CHARLES: What about?

COWPER: About the disaster, of course.

CHARLES: The fire?

COWPER: Yes. Now leave that dummy alone for a few minutes, there's a good boy.

CHARLES: In what capacity do you want these details? As a postman?

COWPER: As an officer of the law. Police-Constable Pogson is engaged with the fire.

CHARLES: I see.

COWPER: When he heard that I was coming this way he asked me to take any particulars from you. I should like to say that as a civil official I have never taken either side in the quarrel that has gone on between this family and the villagers. You may speak quite freely to me.

CHARLES: Thank you.

COWPER: Not at all.

CHARLES: But I have nothing to say.

COWPER: Haven't you?

CHARLES: No. *There is a pause.*

COWPER (*to* JOHN WINTER): Have you anything to say?

WINTER: No.

COWPER: Oh. (*He puts the notebook and pencil back in his pocket*). Well, that's all, then. You can carry on with whatever you were doing. (*He speaks to the villagers.*) I don't know what to do with you. I suppose you can stay here tonight. (*He turns to* CHARLES.) Can they——? What are you laughing at?

CHARLES: You.

COWPER: Is it a laughing matter that the village is destroyed, that the people are wandering homeless, and that the Reverend Mr. Aldus is trapped at the top of the church tower and is roasting like a potato?

CHARLES: Is that why he's ringing the bells?

COWPER: I can tell you, young man, this terrible accident is no laughing matter.

CHARLES: Accident. Was it an accident?

COWPER: Of course. You don't think anybody would do such a thing on purpose?

CHARLES: They might.

COWPER: Don't be silly. Of course it was an accident. I should know—I was there when it started. Complete accident, it was. Just after six o'clock—I was delivering the last post—I was late, I'll admit it, I was late. A letter has just gone into Mr. Aldus's box, and as I was turning away from the door I saw three soldiers coming to the house. The soldiers—you've heard about them?—bit of trouble from them today—nothing that couldn't have been handled with understanding—old soldier myself— but still—there you are. The soldiers had another man with them—a towny fellow, toffed up like. While they passed I hid in the bushes—didn't want to expose myself to any insults while I was in uniform. Anyway, they went straight into Mr. Aldus's house. Just like that— as if they owned it. I could see the four of them talking to Mr. Aldus in his drawing-room—I could see it by the light—by the light of the room. It was the dandy fellow who spoke—talked for about twenty minutes he did and then they came away. I was still hiding as they passed me. The big soldier had his arm around the dandy fellow —and the dandy fellow was talking and talking. I was going to wait until they got from sight before I came out to get on with my round. Then Mr. Aldus came to the door of his house and he must have seen me because he called out, " Cowper, come here ". By the time I'd got to the house he'd gone inside and so I sounded the knocker. He didn't come to the door again, so after a few minutes I went inside. He was in the room with the books and he was carrying armfuls of those books from the shelves and throwing them on the open fire. They were tumbling out from the fireplace into the middle of the room and they were burning, burning away. When I went into the room he stood there for a moment pointing at them and trying to say something, but he couldn't get it out—that stutter of his, you know—and he was crying —crying noisily like a baby. I suppose he wanted me to help him—I don't know really. Anyway, then he went back to carrying more books off the shelves and throwing them on the fire. I was taken aback, I don't mind ad- mitting it. When I'd gathered myself together I ran into the street and began shouting but nobody would come

out—they've been hiding from the soldiers all day. I
ran through the empty streets but there was no one.
When I got back to Mr. Aldus's house the place was afire
and then I heard the bells—he'd gone into the church
and was ringing the bells. The fire spread and nobody
would help me—nobody came out—not even P.C.
Pogson—until they were forced out by the fire. And
now the whole village is destroyed—burned right away.
(*He pauses.*) I hope you think I acted for the best, sir.

CHARLES: What? Yes, I'm sure you did.

COWPER: Thank you, sir. (*He puts on his cap and touches the
peak to* CHARLES.) But what am I doing? I oughtn't to
be here talking. I must get back. Will you let me out,
please?

> JOHN WINTER *opens the window and* THOMAS COWPER
> *goes out by the way he came. There is a murmuring, a
> whispering, from the four old women :* HANNAH
> TREWIN, MARGARET BANT, EDITH TINSON *and*
> FLORA BALDON.

CHARLES: What is it?

EDITH ⎫ (*together*): We saw him.
HANNAH ⎭   We know about the man——

EDITH: You speak, my dear.

HANNAH: No. You speak, my dear.

EDITH: Very well. We saw him.

CHARLES: Who?

HANNAH: The man with the soldiers.

MARGARET: The man who talked so much.

HANNAH: Yes, we saw him.

EDITH: We saw him spoil his beautiful clothes by walking
through the burning streets.

MARGARET: The soldiers followed him—they were laughing,
but he didn't laugh.

EDITH: They came towards us as we ran from the fire.

HANNAH: His white face frightened us.

MARGARET: Yes, it did.

HANNAH: His voice frightened us, too.

MARGARET: Yes.

HANNAH: Long after he'd passed us we could hear it through the sound of the fire.

EDITH: And through the cries of the people.

HANNAH: Even though the bells were ringing.

There is a pause.

FLORA: He spoke to me.

EDITH: No!

HANNAH: Never!

FLORA: Yes, he did.

CHARLES: What did he say? (*She does not answer.*) Well, what did he say?

FLORA: I didn't understand him—I didn't understand what he said—but he spoke to me.

CHARLES: Somewhere here there is a link—— (*He strikes his forehead.*) Think, John Winter, think! (*He leaves the painting and moves about the room.*) What did he say to Paul? What did he say to the old woman? Is it contained in that? I don't know. Perhaps so simple. No, we've missed the moment for discovery. It was when she— (*he points to* FLORA BALDON)—said, " He spoke to me ". Gone now. Never mind. Doesn't matter. (*He returns to the painting, but as an afterthought, says :*) But you, John Winter—would you like to get away? You've time. I'll look after the old man.

WINTER: I'll stay.

CHARLES: All right.

PAUL *has come down the stairs into the room. He is wearing his cloak and carries a hat, a stick and a small case.*

PAUL: John Winter tells me you have given sanctuary to some women of the village.

CHARLES: Yes.

PAUL (*to the villagers*): You are welcome. (*The church bells stop ringing : there is a single bell, then silence. To* CHARLES.) The village is on fire.

CHARLES: Yes.

PAUL: I've been watching the fire from my room.

CHARLES: Have you?

PAUL: It's burning right up—right up into the sky.

CHARLES: Yes.

PAUL: Who is responsible?

CHARLES: It was an accident.

PAUL: There is always the responsibility—it must rest with someone.

WINTER: Mr. Aldus, sir.

PAUL: I remember him.

WINTER: He was burning his books——

PAUL: What's the time?

CHARLES: We don't know. The clock has stopped.

PAUL: I must go soon. I'll wait here. (*He sits down.*) Have you got the cigarettes, John Winter?

WINTER: No, sir. Aren't they in your pocket?

PAUL: I haven't looked. (*He makes no move to do so.*) I just thought I'd like a cigarette whilst I'm waiting. Have you finished the picture, Charles?

CHARLES: Not yet.

PAUL: How long will you be?

CHARLES: I shall work until the last moment.

PAUL: What?

CHARLES: Nothing. I shan't be long.

WINTER: Do you want a cigarette, Mr. Southman?

PAUL: It doesn't matter, John Winter, it doesn't matter. I just thought it would pass the time until I go.

CHARLES: Paul, my dear, listen to me. You must try to remember. You're not going now. Stella is dead——

PAUL: Poor Stella.

CHARLES: —yes, poor Stella—and Procathren has run away and so you are not going to London after all.

PAUL: An excellent statement on the situation, sonny. Very good.

CHARLES: Well you must try to help John Winter and me by remembering these things.

PAUL: I will.

CHARLES: Good. (*He looks down at* STELLA.) Why is her face all sunken? She looks monstrous. Give me that lamp, John Winter.

PAUL: Is it dark out tonight?

WINTER: There's the fire.

PAUL: Of course, the fire. Good. Go and get the axe, John Winter. Also a saw, spades and some rope—we shall want some rope.

WINTER: What are you going to do?

PAUL: Cut down those two trees. Those in front of the house. I told you about them.

WINTER: Yes, you told me, but——

PAUL: What did she call them? She had pet names for them. What were they? I've forgotten. Never mind. We'll have them down—down they shall come. It'll give me something to do—something to occupy me whilst I'm waiting. You think I'm not strong enough. Is that what you think? (*He stands up and strikes* JOHN WINTER *across the face.*) Am I strong enough? Am I? I think so. Get the tools.

CHARLES: Yes, go along, John Winter.

PAUL: Yes, go along. And remember you're a servant. The rope must be strong.   JOHN WINTER *goes out.*

CHARLES: You'd be better employed digging a grave.

PAUL: That's a very unkind thing to say, Charles. Very unkind, indeed. She must be buried, but surely you can't expect a man of my age to go out at night and dig a grave. You must do it with John Winter. I can't do it. You can't expect me to do it—not at my age.

CHARLES: I meant a grave for the dog.

PAUL: Anyway, she can't be buried until you've finished with her. (*He is staring at* STELLA.) Is that blood on her face?

CHARLES: What? No. Paint.

PAUL: Wipe it away.

CHARLES: We musn't touch her.

PAUL: It disfigures her.

CHARLES: It is the death that disfigures her.

PAUL: She would have been glad to know I still intend to go tonight. It was her wish—she was most insistent.

CHARLES: Listen!

PAUL: I'd want to please her, poor dead thing.

CHARLES: Listen to me!

PAUL: I'm going, Stella, just as you wished. (*He laughs.*) Shame on me! Talking to the dead.

CHARLES: Listen to me, Paul.

PAUL: Yes, sonny.

CHARLES: You're not going.

PAUL: No?

CHARLES: Do you hear me? You're not going.

PAUL: Am I not?

CHARLES: No. Procathren's run away. The dinner in your honour has all been eaten up and the guests gone home by now. Whilst they chatted and wondered why you were absent—do you remember what you did?

PAUL: What did I do?

CHARLES: You wandered about this house, a crazy old man, talking of your hey-day.

PAUL: Did I really?

CHARLES: Yes. So you can take off your cloak and put away your hat—you are too late now. It is never going to be.

PAUL: How you run on. Get along with your painting, sonny. (*He calls to the* CHILD.) Come here, little girl. Or are you a little boy? (*The* CHILD *goes slowly to him.*) And what are you called?

CHARLES: Damn you, Paul! God damn you for the beastliness—the selfishness of shutting yourself up in your tower of senility and lunacy at this moment—at this moment!

PAUL: Hush, Charles! You'll frighten the child.

CHARLES: If only I could take refuge in madness as you have done. If only I could convince myself, as you have done, that I am an artist, that the world waited to honour me, that the fires out there were a display for a victory, that these brushes I hold were sceptres and these people princes. Then I might face the future! You have the belief and the refuge—but it is not for me. I cannot go so far. I am not mad. I am not mad. God help me! I can touch the reality and know that I am nothing, that the world censures me, that the fires burn without reason, that these brushes are instruments of torture and these people miserable, frightened clods!

PAUL: Charles, I command you to be quiet! You're frightening this child. (CHARLES *stands quite humbled before the* CHILD'S *penetrating stare*.) Get on with your painting.

CHARLES: Well, try to remember. If you love me, try to remember. Don't pretend.

> CHARLES *returns to the painting.* PAUL *speaks to the* CHILD.

PAUL: Don't let him frighten you. He's afraid—always has been. Poor Charles! Now then—are you going to talk to me for a little while before I go? What shall we talk about? You can talk, can't you? Well, come along, say something to me. Say, " Hullo ". Say my name. Say " Paul ". No? Very well, then, you tell me your name. Haven't you a name? You must have a name. Everyone has a name. Tell it to me for a penny. For twopence, then. Won't you talk to me? Not even for a little while? It can only be for a little while because, you see, I'm going away. Look! I've got my hat—and a stick because I'm very old, and a little case packed with all the things I shall need. Perhaps I should be going now or I shall be late. I wonder what the time is? Ah! you have a watch. What does it say? Let me see. But it has no hands on the face—it's no use at all. Pretty, though. Is that why you wear it? Because it's pretty? I expect so. We don't have pretty things here. I'm sorry. I'd like pretty things and children around me again. Darling, there is one thing I must tell you: I have forgiven you—I have forgiven you. I'm not sad—not really. I'm happy—quite happy. O darling, darling Stella, it's a very great day for me this birthday of mine. There you are—there's something for you to say. Say, " Many happy returns of the day ". (*After a pause the* CHILD *says with great clarity*, Many happy returns of the day.) There! I knew you could speak. Well done! " Many happy returns of the day ", you said. And that is what they will say when I arrive—the great and famous people receiving me—they will say—— (*And*

the little crowd, speaking together, say, Many happy returns of
the day—*and then, possessed by quite a tiny fever of excitement
they cry out separately,* Happy birthday—God bless you
—Much happiness to you *and* Good men are rewarded.
PAUL *standing and holding the hand of the* CHILD *at his side
speaks to her.*) Can you sing? Can you dance? Dance for
me! Dance for me in your lovely gay clothes—as a
birthday gift. Not much to ask. Don't be shy. Look
at me. I'm very old—oh, very old but I can dance and
sing. (*And he does so as the* VILLAGERS *laugh and clap their
hands.* CHRISTIAN MELROSE *has come up the stairs and stands
inside the doorway.* PAUL, *turning and looking beyond the* CHILD,
sees MELROSE *and stops his singing and dancing: the* VIL-
LAGERS *stop their laughter and clapping.*) Have you come
for me?

MELROSE: That's right.

PAUL: I'm ready. Look, I'm quite ready.

MELROSE: Were you expecting me?

PAUL: Oh yes. (*To the* CHILD.) No more dancing now.

> MELROSE *comes fully into the room. The group of women
> give a short scream in unison and gather even closer
> together. The* CHILD *runs to her* MOTHER. *After*
> MELROSE *has entered* KILLEEN *and* CHATER *come in.*

MELROSE: How did you know?

PAUL: I knew.

MELROSE: Who told you I was coming here?

CHARLES: Don't take any notice of him.

MELROSE: Oh, hullo, over there. And why shouldn't I take
any notice of him?

CHARLES: Because he's mad—lunatic.

MELROSE: Is he?

CHARLES: Yes.

MELROSE: Well, mad or not, he's got hold of the right end
of the stick.

CHARLES: About going away?

MELROSE (*yawning*): Yes. God! I'm tired.

CHARLES: Who are you?

MELROSE: That doesn't matter. (KILLEEN *and* CHATER *are*

clowning and fighting in the doorway. MELROSE *turns on them.*)
Stop that! You're Charles Heberden.

CHARLES: Yes.

MELROSE: And that. That's your late, lamented wife?

CHARLES: Yes.

MELROSE: I see. Where's the servant?

CHARLES: Downstairs.

MELROSE: Call him.

CHARLES: I refuse.

MELROSE: Oh, all right. (*To* KILLEEN.) Call him. His name's
Winter. (KILLEEN *goes to the door and calls down the stairs
in a mincing and effeminate way,* Oh Winter; Winter, come
up, please. Your master wants you.) What are these?
He indicates the crowd of villagers.

CHARLES: They're from the village. From the fire. We've
given them shelter.

MELROSE: Quite right, too. I'd better not make a mistake.
This is Paul Southman, isn't it?

CHARLES: Yes.

MELROSE: I shouldn't think there could be two of him. (JOHN
WINTER *comes into the room from below. He is carrying a coil
of rope.*) Ah! Winter?

WINTER: Yes.

MELROSE: Come in. What have you got there?

WINTER: Rope.

MELROSE: I see. Rope.

WINTER: Mr. Southman asked for it.

MELROSE: Asked for it, eh? Chater—Chater, wake up!
Take that. You know what we want. (CHATER *takes the
rope from* JOHN WINTER *and squatting on the floor begins his
work. To* CHARLES.) We thought we'd have to look for
rope. (*He calls to* JOHN WINTER *who is about to go from the
room.*) Hey, you! Winter! Stay here. (*And to* PAUL.)
And you sit down, old man. You're not going yet.

PAUL: Not yet?

MELROSE: No, not for a little while. (PAUL *hesitant, sits—
his hat on his head, and the small bag clutched on his knees.*) Now,
Mr. Heberden——

PAUL: May I talk to the child?

MELROSE: What child? Yes, if you want to. (*He calls to the* CHILD.) Come here, you, and talk to the óld man.

The CHILD *comes forward to stand beside* PAUL.

PAUL: I'm not going yet.

MELROSE has moved to before the painting on the wall.

MELROSE: Your work, Mr. Heberden?

CHARLES: Yes.

PAUL (*to the* CHILD): Won't you talk to me?

MELROSE: It's very beautiful. I suppose I can call it that, can I?

CHARLES: Certainly.

PAUL: (*to the* CHILD): Shall we play a game?

MELROSE: Very beautiful.

PAUL: Shall we ?

MELROSE: Should be in a church.

CHARLES (*he laughs*): Thank you.

MELROSE: What does that mean? Laughing, like that.

CHARLES: Nothing.

PAUL: Crocodiles.

He has taken his spectacles case from his pocket and, removing the spectacles, begins snapping the case at the CHILD'S *nose.*

MELROSE: Is it finished?

CHARLES: No.

MELROSE: Pity.

CHARLES: Yes.

MELROSE: Because it'll never be finished, now, will it?

CHARLES: I suppose not.

MELROSE: Why not?

CHARLES: There won't be time, will there?

MELROSE: That's better—much better! You're beginning to understand. Now we can talk. (*To* CHATER.) How long will you be? (CHATER *stopping his work for a moment, holds up his hand with spread fingers.*) Five minutes? Right. If you'd rather spend those five minutes on your painting, Mr. Heberden——

CHARLES: It doesn't matter.

MELROSE: Sure? O.K.

CHARLES: I should need more than five minutes.

MELROSE: Sorry. Can't give you longer than that. Bobby Procathren should be here by then. I don't know where he's got to. Sit down, Mr. Heberden. (CHARLES *and* MELROSE *sit on the edge of the rostrum : the* VILLAGERS *are grouped together :* PAUL *plays with the* CHILD *:* CHATER, *sitting cross-legged on the floor, the trumpet at his side, is cutting the rope into lengths :* WINTER *and* KILLEEN *stand alone.*) Have a cigarette.

CHARLES: Thank you, I will.   *They light cigarettes.*

PAUL: And it comes along—along—along and snap!

MELROSE: And have some of this.

                    He brings out a bottle of whisky.

CHARLES: No, thank you.

MELROSE: No? Oh, well—— (*He drinks from the bottle throughout the following conversation with* CHARLES.) Are you afraid?

CHARLES: Of course.

MELROSE: You're very young to die. How old are you?

CHARLES: Nearly twenty-one.

MELROSE: I'm thirty-three—but I look older, don't I?

CHARLES: Yes.

MELROSE: I do. I know I do. (*He sees* KILLEEN *among the* VILLAGERS.) Killeen—what are you doing there?

KILLEEN: Nothing! Nothing at all.

MELROSE: Well, come out of it, there's a good boy.

KILLEEN: I wanted to know if they'd got anything to eat.

MELROSE: You can't be hungry. You can't possibly be hungry! You've just had a bloody great meal. (*To* CHARLES.) I don't know, really. Like animals. (*He laughs.*) Perhaps I shouldn't say that. Your cigarette's gone out. Here—let me light it.

CHARLES: Thank you.

PAUL (*to the* CHILD): I was a real Turtle once.

CHARLES: Why are you going to kill us?

MELROSE: Ssh! Keep your voice down. There's no need to frighten the old boy.

CHARLES: You won't do that now. Why are you—you, especially, of all people—going to kill us?

MELROSE: Don't you think I'm capable.

CHARLES: Certainly. I should think so, anyway.

MELROSE: You do?

CHARLES: Yes.

MELROSE: Good. Bobby doesn't think I'm capable. He's dared me to do it. (*He stands up, smiling.*) That's a silly thing to do, isn't it? What does he think I am? What does he think I shall feel? You're nothing to me—neither's the old man. Nobody's anything to me—because there is nobody—hasn't been for years. I care for nothing. They put it right when they said I was an " incorrigible ". Look at me. What do you see?

CHARLES: A monster.

MELROSE: That's through your eyes—and quite natural. I don't take offence. But Bobby can't see me that way. And why? Because he's lived in the world where people —well, where they behave. Where they do this and that for this and that reason—and they do this and that for this and that reason because they have a life to live—a life to plan—and they've got to be careful. That's how he's judging me—that's how he judged you. Silly, isn't it? (*He laughs.*) What am I doing standing up talking like this? I must look a perfect fool!

> *He sits down again beside* CHARLES.

CHARLES: Why should he judge me—or Paul—at all? The fool!

MELROSE: You shouldn't have done it, you know. You've brought this on yourselves. People like us shouldn't do such things to people like that—people who live away out there with women and music. You've struck him very deep. He's talked to me about it and my God! can't he talk. He told me about it, all right. I didn't understand one word in ten about his guilt and the way you've destroyed his innocence—but I understood a little. Poor Bobby!

CHARLES: Why?

MELROSE: He's afraid. Afraid of—what do they call it out there in the world?—hell! it's called by a short, sweet name—I know it as well as my own name—what do they call it?——

CHARLES: I don't know.

MELROSE: Got it! They call it " death ". That's what they call it—death. And that's what he's afraid of.

CHARLES: So that's the corruption beneath the splendour: the maggot in the peacock.

MELROSE: He told Aldus—you know, the clergyman down in the village.

CHARLES: Of course. You went to see Aldus.

MELROSE (*he laughs*): Yes, we saw him. Then he began to burn all his books.

CHARLES: Why?

MELROSE: What?

CHARLES: I asked why he began to burn his books.

MELROSE: Because of what Bobby said to him, I suppose—I don't know.

CHARLES: What did he say?

MELROSE: I've told you—I couldn't understand a blind word. He talked nineteen to the dozen, though. Not only in English but in foreign languages. He took down books and read things out of them. Whatever he said must have been very convincing because he made the padre cry— sat there crying like a baby, he did. I don't wonder. Bobby talked to me—talked until I was drunk with it. I'm so bloody tired as well—we've been on the run for eight days. (MELROSE *sees that the door from below is slowly opening. He calls.*) Who's there? Oh, it's you, Bobby. Come in. We've been waiting for you. (*The door opens fully and* ROBERT PROCATHREN *stands there. His clothes are filthy and torn, his face and hands blackened by the fire.*) Come in. (ROBERT *steps into the room.*) What's the matter? Did you get lost?

ROBERT: I've been sick.

MELROSE: I should say you have. Look, it's all over your coat. Have you eaten too much——

ROBERT: Probably.

MELROSE: —or is it the exercise? Killeen, have you got a handkerchief? Wipe him down.

KILLEEN: I'm a nursemaid—that's what I am.

MELROSE (*to* CHARLES): Bit of a change in him, isn't there? (MELROSE *is exultant, excited by* ROBERT'S *appearance, his degradation.*) Not so beautiful as he was—as we remember him, eh? (*To* ROBERT.) Better now?

ROBERT: Yes. All right, now.

MELROSE: Oh, he's lost that beautiful tie. You've lost your tie, Bobby.

KILLEEN: He gave it to me.

> KILLEEN *is wearing the tie loosely round the neck of his uniform.*

MELROSE: He gave it to you?

KILLEEN: Yes.

MELROSE: Gave it to you?

KILLEEN: Yes!

MELROSE (*laughing*): All right—I'll believe you.

KILLEEN: Well, it's true.

ROBERT: Yes, I gave it to him—as a token.

MELROSE: It's your business.

ROBERT: Melrose.

MELROSE: Yes?

ROBERT: You're not—not " putting it off ", as they say, are you?

MELROSE: No, Bobby, I'm not " putting it off ".

ROBERT: Don't " put it off ", Melrose.

> MELROSE *goes to* ROBERT *and takes* ROBERT'S *face in his hands.*

MELROSE: You think I won't do it, I know. But I'm going to do it.

ROBERT: And what is it you're going to do? Tell me.

MELROSE: You tell me. Ha! It's like a kid's game, isn't it? Who tells who, eh? No, but seriously, Bobby, you tell me. You're the boss from now, you know. You can't get away from it now. If you want to order people like me around you've got to take the responsibility—you've got to. It's always been like that. God knows, I wouldn't have it any other way. But it makes me laugh sometimes. " Melrose do such-and-such! " " Yes, sir! "—and then I look down and see their eyes and their eyes are asking me, " Melrose you think that decision is right, don't you? If you think I'm wrong for God's sake don't do it ". But I do it whatever I think—if I can be bothered to think. What is it I can do for you, Bobby?

ROBERT: Kill the old man and the boy for me.

MELROSE: Just for you. (*There is a pause and then* EDITH TINSON *begins to give short repeated screams.*) What are you doing there, Killeen?

KILLEEN: I'm not doing a thing. I'm not near her. It's not me—it's what he said.

MELROSE: Well, shut her up!

> KILLEEN *goes to the woman and her screams stop. It is then a human voice can be heard humming a polite little tune. It is* CHATER *singing as he works. Now it is apparent what he is doing : from the rope he is constructing two nooses.*

ROBERT: How long?

MELROSE: Not long. (*He grips* ROBERT *by the shoulder : his voice is strong and clear but without anger.*) What have I got to lose in this? Tell me that. Nothing! You're a fool to doubt me, Bobby—a fool! (*Turning, he runs into* KILLEEN.) Get out of the way!

KILLEEN: Hey!

MELROSE: What?

KILLEEN: Do you think there's any food in the place?

MELROSE: For God's sake!——

KILLEEN: Well, some biscuits or something.

MELROSE: There must be something the matter with you.

KILLEEN: I'm thirsty too.

> ROBERT *has moved to stand before* PAUL. *He speaks to him.*

ROBERT: Southman—Southman, can you hear? You're not asleep—you're pretending. Come along, look up. Look up!

MELROSE: Listen! He's beginning to talk to the old man. Quiet, everyone!

ROBERT: Please let me speak.

MELROSE: Carry on, Bobby. Let anyone try to stop you.

ROBERT: You must look at me, Southman.

> PAUL *turns his head.* ROBERT *is now crouched beside him and* PAUL *looks into his face without recognition, without comprehension.*

CHARLES: Leave him alone.

MELROSE (*shouting*): Quiet!

ROBERT: Southman—I thought the power invested was for good. I believed we were here to do well by each other. It isn't so. We are here—all of us—to die. Nothing more than that. We live for that alone. You've known all along, haven't you? Why didn't you tell me—why did you have to teach me in such a dreadful way? For now—(*he cries out*)—I have wasted my inheritance! All these years trying to learn how to live leaving myself such a little time to learn how to die. (*He turns to speak to the* CHILD.) Afraid of the dark? But it is more than the dark. It is that which lies beyond, not within, the dark—the fear of the revelation by light. We are told by our fairy-tale books that we should not fear but the darkness is around us, and our fear is that the unknown hand is already at the switch. I tell you, do not fear, for there is no light and the way is from darkness to darkness to darkness. (PAUL *takes* ROBERT's *hand and holds fast to it.* ROBERT *again speaks to him.*) You old rascal! Knowing it is not a question of finding but of losing the pieties, the allegiances, the loves. You should tell. I've been talking to Aldus. Told him I lost faith in God years ago and never felt its passing. But man—oh, take faith in man from me and the meaning becomes clear by the agony we suffer. What a cost it is. Clear—not for all immediately—no, Aldus is out there at the moment chasing his lost God like a rat down a culvert. But for myself—I am well. (*He moves from* PAUL.) Perhaps I should have understood before coming here. There are many signs out in the world offering themselves for man's comprehension. The flowers in the sky, the sound of their blossoming too acute for our ears leaving us to hear nothing but the clamour of voices protesting, crying out against the end— " It's not fair! "—as they fasten to the walls of life—and the storm is of their own making—it is the howling appeal for tenderness, for love. Only now I see the thing's played out and compassion—arid as an hour-glass—run through. Such matters need not concern us here in this —(*for a moment he is silent*)—in this place. For we have our own flowers to give us understanding. (*He points to* STELLA.) The rose she wears beneath her heart. There, released, is the flower within us all—the bloom that will leap from the breast or drop from the mouth. It shall be my conceit that a flower is our last passport. Who wears it shall go free. Free, Southman!

> *There is a shrill whistle from* CHATER. *He has finished his work and points to two nooses lying coiled on the floor before him.* MELROSE *leaps forward and snatches up the ropes.*

PAUL: John Winter!

ROBERT: Wait!

MELROSE: Ready!

ROBERT: Wait!

PAUL: Let us go.

MELROSE: Yes, come along, old man.

PAUL: I intend to cut down the trees——

ROBERT: Wait!

PAUL: —that stand before the house. They are a danger.

MELROSE: Quite right.

PAUL: You'll help me?

MELROSE: Yes.

PAUL: Are the tools there, John Winter?

MELROSE: Let him believe it. Come on, let him believe it!

WINTER: The tools are at the door, sir.

PAUL: I see you have the rope.

MELROSE: Yes, I have the rope.

PAUL: Good.

MELROSE: Killeen, take Mr. Southman down.

KILLEEN: Right-o.

PAUL: Thank you.

> PAUL *and* KILLEEN *go out and down the stairs.*

MELROSE: Chater, bring Mr. Heberden. (CHATER *takes* CHARLES'S *arm.*) Oh, by the way, you're not a religious man or anything?

CHARLES: No.

MELROSE: What I mean is, do you want to say goodbye to your wife?

CHARLES: No.

MELROSE: Go along, then. (CHATER *and* CHARLES *go out and down the stairs.*) What are you going to do, Winter?

WINTER: I don't know.

MELROSE: Any ideas?

WINTER: Go away, I suppose.

MELROSE: Have you anywhere to go?

WINTER: No.

> MELROSE *takes some bank-notes from his pocket. He separates several and holds them out to* JOHN WINTER.

MELROSE: Here, take this.

WINTER: Oh, thank you, sir. Thank you.

MELROSE: That's all right. (JOHN WINTER *takes the money and hurries away by the stairs to the upper part of the house.* ROBERT *moves to* STELLA'S *body and stands looking down at her. There is silence. Suddenly* MELROSE *speaks.*) Ready?

ROBERT (*immediately*): Ready.

> MELROSE *and* ROBERT *go out and down the stairs. When they have gone there is a pause and then the* CHILD, *detaching herself from the group of* VILLAGERS, *moves across the room to where* STELLA'S *body lies. The* CHILD *stares from above at the dead face and, extending a finger, touches for a moment the closed eyes. It is then the* MOTHER *calls to the* CHILD.

JUDITH: Stella! (*Startled by the call the* CHILD *stumbles among the bones and so moves from the body. In doing so she accidentally knocks against the table and cries out in pain.*) Stella, dear child! (*But the* CHILD *moves on and seeing the green scarf,*

CHARLES'S *present to* PAUL, *lying on the floor, she picks it up and puts it around her neck.*) Stella! We are strangers here, Stella.

The CHILD *takes up the copy of " Alice in Wonderland " from the table. The trumpet suddenly sounds from the garden : a raucous tune. The* CHILD, *with the book in her hand, performs a grave dance to the music. As abruptly as it began the trumpet stops. The* CHILD'S *dance continues for a little but she hesitates, listening. There is no sound. Dropping the book to the floor she runs to her* MOTHER *and hides her face in the woman's lap. There is no sound and everything is still : quite still.*

CURTAIN